MEMORY MAKERS

CREATIVE
PAPER TECHNIQUES
for SCRAPBOOKS

More than 75 fresh paper craft ideas

MEMORY
MAKERS
BOOKS

Executive Editor Kerry Arquette   **Founding Editor** Michele Gerbrandt

---

Editor MaryJo Regier

Art Director Andrea Zocchi

Craft Director Pam Klassen

Photographer Ken Trujillo

Idea Editor Janetta Wieneke

Graphic Artist Nick Nyffeler

Hand Model Erikia Ghumm

Contributing Writers Kelly Angard, Lori Elkins Solomon, Anne Wilbur

Contributing Photographers Marc Creedon, Christina Dooley, Brenda Martinez

Featured Artists See Artist Index on page 127

Editorial Support Dena Twinem

Memory Makers® Creative Paper Techniques for Scrapbooks

Published by Memory Makers Books, an imprint of F+W Publications, Inc.
First edition. Printed in the United States.

11 10 09 08 07   11 10 9 8 7

Library of Congress Cataloging-in-Publication Data

Creative paper techniques for scrapbooks : more than 75 fresh paper craft ideas /
Memory Makers.
    p. cm.
Includes bibliographical references and index.
ISBN-13: 978-1-892127-21-1 (pbk. : alk. paper)
ISBN-10: 1-892127-21-0 (pbk. : alk. paper)
1. Paper work. 2. Scrapbooks. I. Memory Makers

TT870 C747 2002
745.54—dc21

2002032601

fw
F+W PUBLICATIONS, INC.

Distributed to trade and art markets by
F+W Publications, Inc.
4700 East Galbraith Road, Cincinnati, OH 45236
Phone 1-800-289-0963

Memory Makers Books is the home of *Memory Makers*, the scrapbook magazine dedicated to educating and inspiring scrapbookers. To subscribe, or for more information, call 1-800-366-6465.
Visit us on the Internet at www.memorymakersmagazine.com.

This book belongs to

We dedicate this book to all of our *Memory Makers* contributors whose imaginative and delightful paper craft ideas are the inspiration behind this book.

TABLE OF CONTENTS

18

61

76

116

Sibling Revelry

Trying to take the perfect picture is an exercise in patience, and you have to have a lot of film!

Anna, Sasha and Daniel 2002

Sibling Revelry (See page 126)

INTRODUCTION
The colors, textures and patterns of paper continually stimulate our senses. You may love to look at paper, but, if you're like me, you also have to touch it. I like to feel the thickness, flexibility, and run my thumb across the surface texture. From my first fold-and-cut paper snowflakes made as a child, to the sophisticated folds in my scrapbooks today, paper's diversity simply fascinates me.

Paper and paper crafts have been around for thousands of years, across all cultures, and yet new paper crafts continue to emerge and find their way into our lives and into our scrapbooks. I am very excited about this book for many reasons.

This is a paper experience that will change forever the way you look at scrapbook papers! It features a wide array of easy-to-make paper craft projects that use simple, basic tools and supplies that you probably already own. No prior creative training is needed and the projects are well-suited for scrapbookers of all skill levels—so there's something for everyone!

Each project is accompanied by step-by-step illustrations. Most projects use specific patterned papers, templates and other basic supplies to teach the techniques. But our aim is to encourage individual experimentation. The true beauty of these paper craft techniques is that once you learn the basics, you can apply these techniques to your favorite scrapbook papers in colors that coordinate with your photos. We provide useful suggestions for helping you do just that! In addition, there are reproducible patterns and drawings to assist you in making these projects. The final *Gallery* section presents an array of gorgeous spinoffs of these techniques to further inspire you!

Who would've ever thought that a simple sheet of paper could be transformed into such a textural enhancement for your scrapbooks! I hope you will enjoy this book and will be inspired to experiment with your own scrapbook papers and these wonderful techniques. So go on, take a piece of paper and hold it. Turn it over in your hand. Fold it, cut it, tear it and create!

Michele

Michele Gerbrandt
Founding Editor
Memory Makers® magazine

PAPER 101

The economical prices and widespread availability of scrapbook papers—in hundreds of colors, patterns, textures and weights—make paper crafting all the more enjoyable. However, paper for scrapbooks should be both fun and functional. To be photo-safe, paper should be pH neutral (acid-free) and lignin-free. Many paper varieties are also buffered, which is preferable for scrapbooking projects. The paper techniques featured in this book use specific paper products, but each is easily adaptable to your favorite scrapbook paper types and patterns.

Be aware that while they are beautiful to look at, not all vellum, mulberry, metallic or handmade papers are of archival quality and as such, should not be allowed to directly touch photos and memorabilia. Have fun experimenting with a variety of different papers and you will soon see that contrast between the different paper types can greatly enhance the effect of a project.

Types of paper

Metallic Shiny, metallic papers—some holographic—are available in many colors. Use these for replicating page accents of metallic objects such as picture frames or when a little sparkle and sheen are desired.

Handmade Reminiscent of old-fashioned, rough-textured paper, its fibers, confetti and other elements add visual impact to paper art.

Mulberry Papers with a heavy look of wood fiber; useful for pages and paper projects calling for a natural, outdoorsy feel.

Suede A leathery-looking paper, available in a number of colors, which is useful for adding texture to paper crafts.

Vellum Transparent paper, either solid-colored or patterned, that is great for decorative elements where a sheer effect is desired.

Cardstock Sturdier paper, available in a multitude of colors and patterns, which is especially useful for backgrounds, matting photos and making paper photo frames.

Solid-colored paper Basic solid papers, available in hundreds of colors and a variety of weights, can be used alone or with any other paper type.

Patterned paper Multi-use, versatile paper that can support theme layouts and is available in hundreds of different designs and patterns.

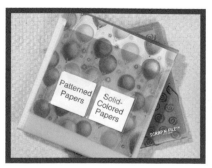

Proper paper storage Protect your investment by treating your paper with care. Keep it out of the sun and away from moisture. Store the sheets flat if possible or upright in a container made specifically for storing paper, such as a Scrap-N-File™ (Caren's Crafts).

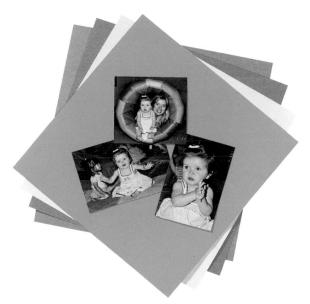

Selecting paper colors based on photos

Color affects our thoughts and emotions as well as the outcome of our scrapbook pages. Some colors (red) inspire energetic feelings while others (blue and green) are calming. When selecting paper colors for your scrapbook pages, choose shades that are consistent with the mood of your photos.

Another successful strategy is to draw colors and patterns from your photos. You may wish to pick up on the blue in the background sky, or the green of grass, the color or pattern of an outfit or the hue of a person's eyes. Once you determine a primary color, choose other colors that complement your primary choice.

If you aren't confident about choosing colors, consider buying papers in presorted packages. These packets come with corresponding, coordinating papers in color and theme variations. Prepackaged papers help take the guesswork out of paper selection.

Can't figure out what colors to use? Pick up a color wheel at your local art or craft store. A color wheel has a rotating dial that helps users choose colors that work together harmoniously. The wheel shows complementary colors (colors that fall directly opposite each other on the wheel, such as green and red) and other combinations. There are dozens of ways to use the color wheel when scrapbooking.

Determining paper grain All machine-made paper is easier to fold or tear in one direction than in the other because the paper consists of parallel fibers, called "the grain." Working against the grain can give uneven and ragged results, which is fine if that is the look you desire. For crisp folds and smoothly torn edges, go with the grain. Experiment with sample scraps from your scrapbook papers to learn how to identify the grain as we have done below. Then use this knowledge to your advantage when creating your paper art.

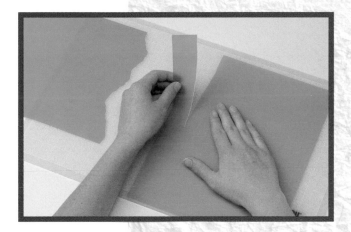

Tearing paper When paper—in this case vellum—is torn against the grain, it creates uneven and ragged tears as shown on the left. Likewise, when the same vellum is torn with the grain, the result is a predictable tear.

Folding paper The square of patterned paper at the top of the example above was folded against the grain, resulting in a rough fold. When the same paper is folded with the grain, a clean, crisp fold is created.

TOOLS & SUPPLIES

Use this list of tools and supplies to help you get started in these exciting and creative paper techniques. You'll find that you probably already have most of the "basic" tools listed. These are tools that you will need for most any paper craft project. The "optional" tools listed on the next page are tools used in various projects featured in this book. While it is not essential that you have these tools to make specific projects, they can certainly make the job easier. Tips and techniques for using tools follow on pages 12 through 14.

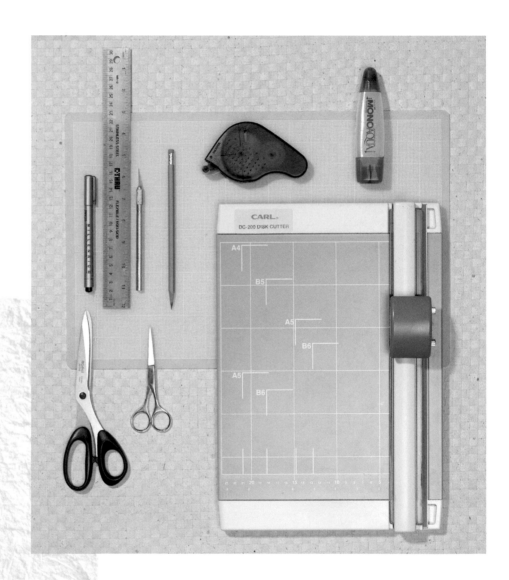

The Basics
- Craft knife
- Cutting mat
- Liquid adhesive
- Metal straightedge ruler
- Pencil
- Personal paper trimmer
- Pigment pens
- Regular scissors
- Small scissors
- Tape adhesive

Your workspace For successful paper crafting, keep your workspace clean and organized. Regularly remove any adhesive residue from your cutting mat and tools. Keep basic tools handy, as you will use them the most.

Optional tools

- Art Deckle™ ruler
- Bone folder
- Embellishments (beads, buttons, wire, etc.)
- Embossing stylus
- Graph paper
- Graphing ruler
- Letter templates
- Memorabilia keepers
- Metal flakes
- Nested templates
- Paper crimper
- Quilling needle, slotted quilling needle & paper strips
- Removable artist tape
- Rubber stamps & inkpad
- Shape punches
- Small paintbrush
- Spoon
- Tweezers
- Vellum adhesive

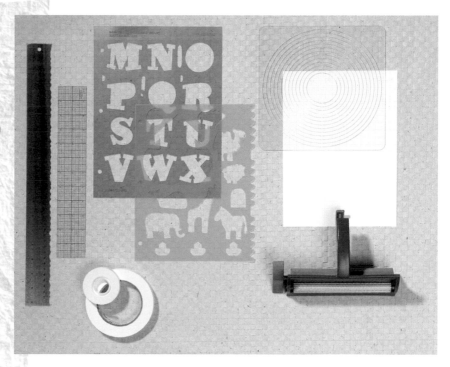

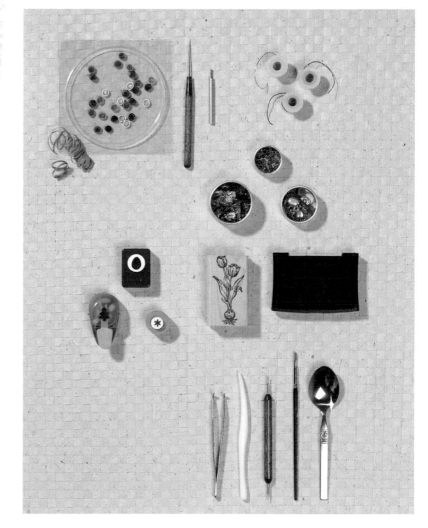

Mounting paper projects in scrapbooks
For longevity, we recommend the use of acid- and lignin-free albums and paper products, archival-quality adhesives, PVC-free plastics and pigment inks for journaling.

ILLUSTRATED TIPS & TECHNIQUES

These illustrated tips and techniques will help you achieve the best possible results from your paper, tools and supplies. Begin with a work surface that is clean and protected by a self-healing cutting mat. A self-healing cutting mat does not become pitted by craft knife cuts, ensuring that new paper cuts will always go where you put them. Make sure your tools are clean and dry. Replace any cutting blades and sharpen the edges of scissors on a whetstone, if needed, before you begin any paper craft project.

Cutting with a craft knife For straight cuts, hold the craft knife against the edge of a ruler. Use a craft knife to cut in tiny areas where scissors can't reach. Cut into cardstock at an angle to prevent white backing from showing through.

Cutting against a metal straightedge ruler When cutting straight lines, cut against a metal straightedge ruler with a nonskid backing instead of a plastic graphing ruler, which the knife will cut into. Hold paper and ruler firmly to prevent slipping.

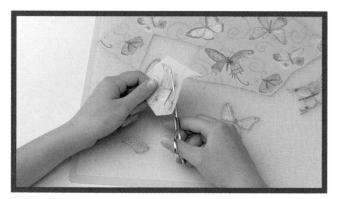

Cutting with scissors Scissors should be clean and sharp. For precision, small scissors work best when silhouette-cropping elements from paper. Use long strokes with larger scissors to ensure a smooth-cut line.

Cutting with a paper trimmer Paper trimmers are great for making perfectly straight cuts and for cutting your own quilling strips. Hold paper firmly in place with left hand, then lower or slide the blade down quickly and smoothly.

Anchoring a work in progress Hold artwork down while you are working on it, particularly when weaving on a loom, with low-tack, removable artist tape. The tape will remove easily without marring the paper surface or leaving residue behind.

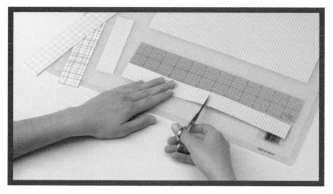

Measure twice, cut once When cutting paper strips or blocks for a project that requires evenly sized, accurate strips, follow the golden rule of carpentry and quilting: Measure twice and cut once.

Measuring with a graphing ruler A graphing ruler can be used with a pencil to mark grids or cutting lines on the back of paper. You can easily view the paper surface beneath the ruler's clear surface for accurate measuring when needed.

Marking placement guides Use a pencil and ruler to draw guidelines to help you accurately place vertical or horizontal paper strips for weaving, for evenly spaced punching, etc.

Making a pattern Make a freehand cut or template-traced pattern on cardstock. Strive for accuracy—a well-made pattern provides the best results. Label pattern with solid lines for cut lines and dotted lines for fold lines.

Transferring a pattern to paper Transfer patterns to paper directly from the source on a light box, with tracing paper or against a sunny window. To size a pattern to fit your page, use a photocopier; print the resized image directly on paper or transfer it by hand.

Scoring against a metal straightedge ruler When folding cardstock or mulberry paper, use a metal straightedge ruler and a bone folder to "score" the paper first where you will place the fold. This will make it easier to achieve a crisp fold.

Creating a crisp fold After scoring the paper with a bone folder—made of real bone or plastic—fold the paper on the score and then rub the bone folder along the length of the fold to flatten the crease into a crisp, finished fold.

Flattening a fold Turn your finished, folded art over and rub a spoon along all fold lines to flatten out the folds on the backside. This will give the front of your art a flat, smooth appearance.

Controlling a tear Different papers tear differently; some tear clean, others ragged. For greatest control, tear between the finger and thumbnails. Practice tearing a wide variety of papers to learn what to expect from each paper type.

Using a Deckle ruler for tearing For uniform and straight tears, try using tearing paper against the edge of a Deckle ruler, which works well for tearing soft papers such as mulberry and vellum.

Using needle for tightly quilled centers A slotted needle is a quick-and-easy tool to use for quilling, but only a needle or hatpin will give you a very tightly coiled "peg." Dampen the end of paper strip to help it stick to the needle for rolling.

Tearing quilling strip ends Before rolling a quilling strip into a coil, tear one end. Insert the straight, untorn end into the slotted needle and coil. Apply adhesive to the torn end of the finished coil for a "seamless" finish.

1

CUTTING

When you lovingly cut out your first valentine as a child, you ventured into the centuries-old craft of paper cutting. Paper cutting originated in China approximately 1500 years ago, and the art form has been passed on from generation to generation and across many cultures. Numerous forms of single- and multiple-layer paper cutting are apt and suitable techniques for scrapbook pages. In this section, you will discover how to:

- *Create pull-apart borders and backgrounds using decorative rulers, templates and freeform designs*
- *Cut apart and reassemble paper to create multidimensional designs*
- *Create free-form, pull-apart alphabets*
- *Add relief detail to template-cut shapes*
- *Cut multicolored, layered designs utilizing a single pattern*
- *Create intricate designs through silhouette cropping*

Paper cutting is the foundation of many other creative paper techniques. Master these basics and then combine them with the other amazing techniques featured in later chapters.

SINGLE-LAYER CUTTING

Single-layer cutting is the very foundation of creative paper techniques. Cut a simple sheet of paper with scissors or a craft knife, and it is transformed into a versatile page embellishment. Create a variety of borders and backgrounds by experimenting with decorative rulers and templates. Or create freeform designs using just your imagination and creative muse for single-layer cut paper designs with lots of impact.

Cynthia Anning

Pull apart a shaped border

Add pizazz to a border using a decorative ruler to draw lines and then cut paper into strips in a variety of widths. Changing the design of the decorative ruler and placing your borders at the upper or lower edges of the page will give you a completely different look. Follow the steps on the next page to create border; mount on page. Single and double mat photos. Freehand cut waterdrop designs. Print title lettering on computer and then crop and mat.

What you will need

- Two sheets of coordinating, solid-colored papers

- Decorative ruler (Creative Memories)

- Computer front (Creating Keepsakes)

1 Draw two parallel lines ¼" apart using a decorative ruler to form the cutting guidelines.

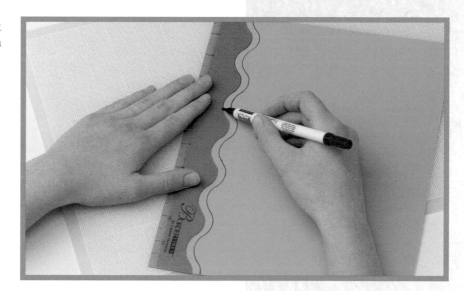

2 Cut along the drawn guide-lines with a pair of scissors or use a craft knife (if the decorative ruler you use has a more linear pattern), forming two strips of paper.

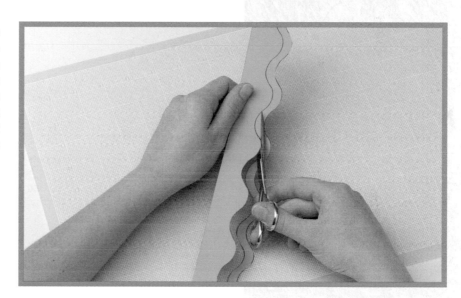

3 Mount strips onto background paper, pulling them apart to leave ¼" space between the two to allow background paper to show through.

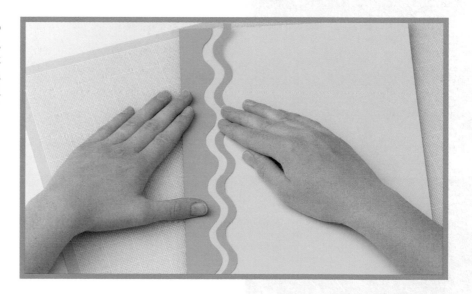

Use a template to create a pull-apart design

Create visual interest using a simple template design by cutting out the shape, pulling it apart, and then mounting all the segments on background paper, leaving space between each piece. Change the template shape to coordinate with your page and photo themes, if desired. Follow the steps on page 19 before triple matting design. Circle cut photos; mount on page. Add journaling at center and title phrase around edge of second matting.

Kelly Angard; Photos Torrey Miller

What you will need

- Two to four sheets of coordinating, solid-colored papers

- Leaf template (Fiskars)

- Circle shape cutter or circle template

1 On paper of choice, position and trace template shape; draw two parallel lines about ¼" apart, connecting the drawn shapes and forming continuous cutting lines.

2 Using small, sharp scissors, cut along drawn lines, making sure to use one continuous stroke of the scissors for a clean cut. Similar to silhouette cropping, have patience and move the paper in and out of the scissor blades instead of moving the blade around the shape.

3 Place the five cut-apart segments in order on complementary-colored background paper, making sure to pull segments apart to allow background paper to show through. Adhere segments. Turn page over and trim off any overlap of the segmented pieces.

Pull apart a free-form background

Draw your own freehand design to be cut, pulled apart, and then reassembled to complement the theme of your photos. Follow the steps on the next page to create the animal-print background design shown here. Try this technique for creating zoo, flag, beach, landscape or rainbow backgrounds—or any theme where a wavy pattern is desired. Freehand draw and cut paw prints; crop photos to fit. Circle cut smaller photos and mat on black paper. Adhere sticker letters and paw-print stickers. Complete page with journaling.

Lorna Christensen

What you will need
- Two sheets of coordinating, solid-colored papers
- One sheet black paper
- White pencil
- Sticker letters (Provo Craft)
- Paw-print stickers (Creative Memories)

1 Freehand draw striped animal pattern on backside of solid-colored paper.

2 Photocopy drawn paper or number the stripes sequentially to make reassembly easier, if desired. Use scissors to cut along the drawn lines; set aside pieces in their proper order.

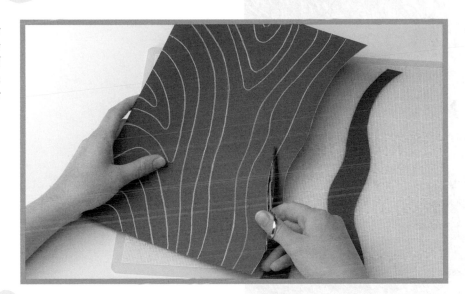

3 Reassemble pieces in order with front side showing (your pattern will be a reverse image of what you drew) onto complementary-colored background paper, making sure to leave space between each piece so the background paper shows through. You may not be able to use all of the outer stripes depending on how much space you leave between the stripes. Finally, trim off any overlap.

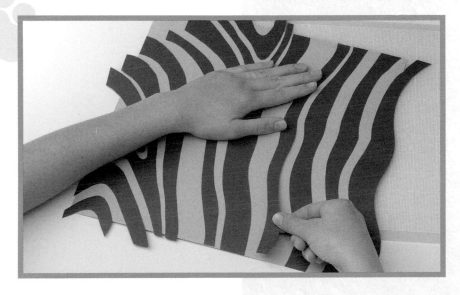

Add depth to patterned paper pull-aparts

Take patterned paper to a new dimension by slicing random segments and layering with self-adhesive foam spacers. Follow the steps on page 23 to create a background with depth. Double mat background design. Double mat photos; round corners and trim one with decorative scissors. Create title letters with template and patterned paper, mat and silhouette crop. Mount on vellum trimmed with decorative scissors and triple mat. Layer photos and title block on page, tucking corners under slices layered with foam spacers. Cut two 10" pieces of craft wire, twist a loop at one end with needle-nose pliers, add beads and twist second end to hold beads in place. Repeat process in random fashion, adding curves, loops and beads. Secure to page with flexible adhesive.

What you will need

- Two duplicate sheets of patterned paper (Creative Imaginations)

- Three sheets of coordinating, solid-colored papers

- Vellum (Strathmore)

- Decorative scissors (Fiskars)

- Corner rounder punch

- Self-adhesive foam spacers

- Lettering template (EK Success)

- Wire (Artistic™ Wire)

- Beads (Westrim)

- Needle-nose pliers

- Flexible adhesive (Glue Dots International)

Kelly Angard

1 Begin with two sheets of the same patterned paper. Slice one sheet along design lines; set the other aside.

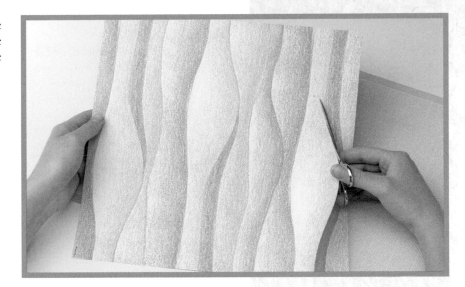

2 Reassemble slices onto solid-colored paper, leaving space between each slice so that the background shows through.

3 Slice selected segments from second sheet of patterned paper. Adhere onto first sheet of patterned paper atop same pattern lines with self-adhesive foam spacers.

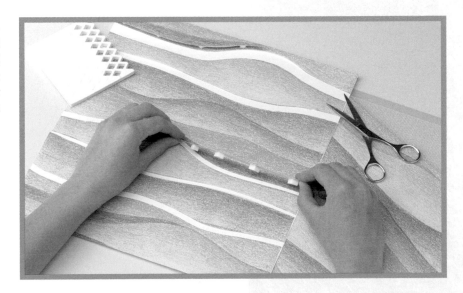

Pull apart some title letters

Chopping-block title lettering gives your page a "woodsy" look—especially when cut from interesting patterned papers. Cut title letters from paper squares as shown on the next page. Adhere to background paper. Single and double mat photos. Add pen detail and journaling. Punch leaves; add to drawn vine and randomly scatter on page.

Two little squirrels sittin' in the leaves...

The answer my friend is blowin' in the wind...

Hey! Look at that big purple le

Joanna Navone

One crisp day in October, Meg & Brie decided to help Mark with the leaves.....

Peek-a-boo!

'98

What you will need

- Scraps of coordinating solid-colored papers
- Pencil
- Leaf punches (Emagination Crafts)

1 Cut patterned paper into 1 x 1" squares. Freehand draw or trace letters lightly with a pencil, exaggerating some letters to make sure your pencil lines extend to the outside edges of the square. Cut on lines with scissors. Reassemble pieces on page, leaving space between to allow background paper to show through. Practice straight letters, such as E, L and Y before tackling rounded letters like B, R and S.

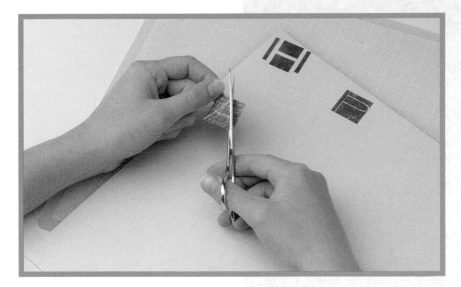

MULTIPLE-LAYER CUTTING

Cutting multiple layers of paper provides a myriad of ways to add shape, dimension and color to a scrapbook page. Each time you add a layer to your page, you add new possibilities to your design. Simple template shapes become more lifelike, and the designs in patterned paper almost seem to pop off the page. Each cut you make becomes an irresistible window offering a peek at the layers of paper below.

Jodi Amidei

What you will need

- Five to six sheets of coordinating, solid-colored papers
- Shape template (Provo Craft)
- Lettering template (Daisy Doodle)
- Pencil
- Small swirl punch (All Night Media)

Add detail to template shapes

Give template shapes dimension by cutting or punching details and designs before layering over complementary background paper. Follow the steps on page 27 to create unique template designs. Triple mat photo and add pen stroke detail. Tear solid-colored paper for earthen border; add pen stroke details. Layer photo and template shapes on page. Create title letters with template, mat and silhouette crop before adding pen stroke detail.

1 Select two solid-colored papers for each template shape to be used. Trace template shape on both sheets of paper and cut out. Select one of the two colored shapes for the top layer; set the other aside.

2 Use a metal straightedge ruler and a pencil to draw details on shape. A freehand design may also be drawn onto template shape as shown on the giraffe.

3 Use a craft knife to cut out drawn design. Another option to cutting a design with a craft knife is to punch a design, as shown on the sheep. Layer cut or punched shape over second shape previously set aside, with either flat adhesive or self-adhesive foam spacers for added dimension.

Cut details into layered design

A hand-cut and layered design is an exquisite feature that can complement the theme of your photos. Follow the steps on the next page to create the leaf design shown here. Use your own pattern or template shape to match your page theme. Crop photos into ovals, mat and layer on page. Create title block by double matting paper rectangles slightly askew. Adhere sticker letters and complete with journaling and pen detail.

'LEAF' IT TO US!

Like most kids, Cami & Evan love raking leaves in the fall! of course, jumping into the big piles is the most fun!

Stacey Shigaya

What you will need

- One sheet of patterned paper (Paper Adventures)

- Two sheets of coordinating solid-colored papers (The Crafter's Workshop)

- Pattern on page 124

- Oval shape cutter or oval template

- Sticker letters (Making Memories)

1 Photocopy and size pattern provided onto regular white paper to fit your scrapbook page. Place pattern onto foreground paper of choice, positioning where you want the cut image to be. Tack paper down with removable artist tape to hold in place, if desired. Use a craft knife and steady hands to carefully cut out tiny shapes.

2 Select a sheet of solid-colored paper for the second layer; place it beneath cut foreground paper. Adhere together to prevent the paper from sliding when cutting. Using cut foreground paper as a pattern, carefully cut out shapes just a bit smaller than those cut on the foreground paper so that the second layer shows through the first.

3 Select a third sheet of solid-colored paper for the third and final background layer. To assemble, layer cut foreground and middle sheets atop background layer and adhere.

Cut peek-a-boo layers into patterned paper

Patterned papers provide a variety of options for cutting out details and layering for one-of-a-kind works of art. Follow the instructions below to create the layered border shown here. Then double mat smaller photos and mat large photo on patterned paper, torn and crumpled for texture, with self-adhesive foam spacers; mat again. Print title and journaling from computer; cut to size. Adhere fiber along top of page; mount title squares over fiber, leaving space for fiber to show through.

What you will need

- Two duplicate sheets of patterned paper in different colors (EK Success, Magenta)

- One sheet of coordinating-color, striped patterned paper (EK Success)

- Two sheets coordinating solid-colored papers

- Craft fiber (On the Surface)

- Self-adhesive foam spacers

- Computer font (Hallmark's Scrapbook Studio)

Brandi Ginn

1 Select two patterned papers in contrasting colors to cut designs from and layer with each other. Slice a 2½" strip from each sheet of paper for the border. Using a craft knife, cut along paper's natural design lines for first layer. Mount over second 2½" strip of paper in contrasting color; cut design into lower layer a little bit smaller than original cuts. Depending upon your eye, you may want to pencil in the design to cut on the second layer. Assemble and adhere the two cut layers with self-adhesive foam spacers atop a third border strip that is 2¾" wide. Mount completed border down side of background paper.

Cut and layer a self-framing background

Geometric designs on patterned paper provide perfect lines for cutting, layering and reassembling with foam spacers to create a self-framing background. Follow the steps on page 32 to create a layered background from a single sheet of paper. Insert fiber-accented photo, sliding it beneath the innermost layers, and adhere in place. Cut title letters from template and solid-colored paper; mount on title block and add journaling. Insert title block beneath innermost layers next to photo and adhere.

Pamela Frye; Photo Lois Duncan

What You Will Need

- One sheet of patterned paper (Memory Muse Designs)
- Two sheets of coordinating, solid-colored paper
- ⅛" and ¼" self-adhesive foam spacers
- Fiber
- Lettering template (C-Thru Ruler Co.)

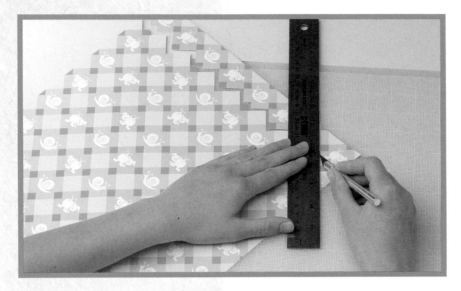

1 Use a craft knife and metal straightedge ruler to cut below the top row of diamond shapes, resulting in a border strip. Cut a second strip from the top of paper in the same manner. Repeat on the lower edge of the paper, resulting in four border strips. If your paper's design allows, you can also do this down the side edges to create side borders.

2 Adhere center section of diamond-shaped paper in the center of a sheet of solid-colored background paper. Use 1/8" self-adhesive foam spacers to reassemble and adhere one upper and one lower border strip next to the center section.

3 Use 1/4" self-adhesive foam spacers to reassemble and adhere the remaining upper and lower border strips in place next to those adhered in Step 2.

Cut and layer an elegant title page

Create a stunning title page with elaborately patterned paper cut and layered three times for a multidimensional work of art. While this patterned paper has a very specific design, you can use this technique on any patterned paper with an elegant, baroque, old-world botanical or antique textile print. Follow the steps on page 34 to create this design. Freehand draw and cut title banners; outline with pen and write title. Mount with self-adhesive foam spacers.

A Celebration of Love

25ᵗʰ Anniversary

Kelly Angard

What you will need

- Two duplicate sheets of patterned paper (NRN Designs)

- Two sheets of coordinating solid-colored papers

- Self-adhesive foam spacers

1 Trim dark gray border away from patterned paper in one continuous cut; set aside (not shown). Silhouette crop elements from the corners of the first sheet of patterned paper, following natural design lines. Using a craft knife, cut out a large design "medallion" from the center of the same sheet of patterned paper (not shown).

2 Adhere solid-colored papers behind the openings in detached corner pieces and center medallion of patterned paper. Trim off any excess overlap and set pieces aside.

3 One-eighth of an inch in from the edges of a solid-colored sheet of background paper, center and adhere the trimmed gray border from Step 1. Reassemble and layer cut and matted elements atop second sheet of patterned background paper, placing pieces over their original positions with self-adhesive foam spacers.

2

CUTTING & FOLDING

Picture the simple elegance of a Chinese paper fan, and you can easily understand the decorative impact that can be created by paper cutting and folding. Cutting and then folding paper adds depth and texture to a scrapbook page. Here you will learn to:

- *Turn folded paper strips into lovely, window-style "louvers"*
- *Piece together a number of varieties of bargello quilts*
- *Accent photos with a paper technique inspired by a camera lens' shutter opening—the iris fold*
- *Pinch paper to create pleats borrowed from the world of sewing*

Patience and creativity are all that's needed to master these simple but stunning techniques. With every cut and fold you make, you'll add a touch of elegance to your pages.

LOUVERS

Like the interior design accents from which this paper technique draws its inspiration, "louvers" are single-folded strips of paper that are used to fill in a cut-out "window" on your page. By varying the patterns, textures and directions of the paper strips, you can create a variety of showcases for your photos. Tuck the corners of photos, journaling blocks and memorabilia behind the strips for a truly unique scrapbook display.

Brandi Ginn

Create horizontal louvers to feature photos

The practical, linear design of a horizontal louver mat creates an interesting and useful display for photos. Patterned papers add visual impact. For a 12 x 12" page, start by trimming a 12 x 12" sheet of solid-colored cardstock down to 11¼" wide x 10¼" tall. Then cut out a 9¼" W x 8¼" T rectangular "window" opening to create a 1" wide frame; set frame aside. Follow the steps on page 37 to create cut-and-fold paper louvers. Mat photos; tuck under louvered strips and adhere. Print title and journaling on vellum; cut in blocks or to size, then mat and mount on page.

What you will need

- Two to five monochromatic, coordinating patterned papers (Making Memories)
- One sheet coordinating, solid-colored cardstock for frame
- Bone folder
- Vellum
- Computer fonts (*Boyz R Gross* downloaded from Internet; *LD Going Nuts* Inspire Graphics)

1 Begin by slicing sixteen 2" wide strips from different patterned papers. On the backside of each paper strip, use a metal straightedge ruler as a guide to run a bone folder down the center of each strip lengthwise to score a fold line (see page 13).

2 Fold each strip on the scored line with wrong sides pressed together, pressing along the fold with bone folder to form the louver strips.

3 Apply adhesive to the inner edges of the back side of the frame. Mount folded louver strips horizontally across the frame's opening, overlapping strips about ½". Work from the top down and bottom up, keeping the folds pointed inward, toward the center of the frame. Continue until the frame opening is louvered.

Make a diagonal louver variation

Diagonal louvers, such as these within a stamped and embossed window frame, provide visual variation for nestling photos and memorabilia. For a 12 x 12" page, trim down one sheet of cardstock to 11¼ x 11¼"; cut a 8¾ x 8¾" opening to form frame. Stamp and emboss images on frame. Mat frame with second color of cardstock; cut out center opening, leaving ⅛" edge showing behind the top frame. Cut twenty 2" strips of white or cream-colored paper, then follow steps on page 37 to score and fold louvers. Apply adhesive to the inner edges of the backside of the frame. Mount louver strips on the diagonal, overlapping strips ½". Layer strips, beginning at the center and working out toward corners in both directions. Mat photos and journaling block; layer and tuck along with memorabilia beneath louvers. Cut title letters from template; punch holes for letter details. Double mat and layer with self-adhesive foam spacers.

Torrey Miller

What you will need

- Two sheets of coordinating, solid-colored cardstock for matted frame

- One to two sheets of white or cream-colored paper for louvers

- Rubber stamps (Hero Arts, Stampin' Up), embossing ink (Ranger), embossing powder (Stampendous)

- Bone folder

- Lettering template (Scrap Pagerz)

- Hole punch

- Self-adhesive foam spacers

Frame a photo with textured louvers

Crimped, patterned vellum, folded and mounted as louver strips on frame, provides a delicate, textured touch to portraits. Begin by mounting photo on background paper. Follow the instructions below to create the louvered layers. Cut two 1 x 8" strips of embossed card stock; mount horizontally above and below portrait. Print title on patterned paper; silhouette cut. Print journaling on vellum; layer over patterned paper and mount on page with eyelets.

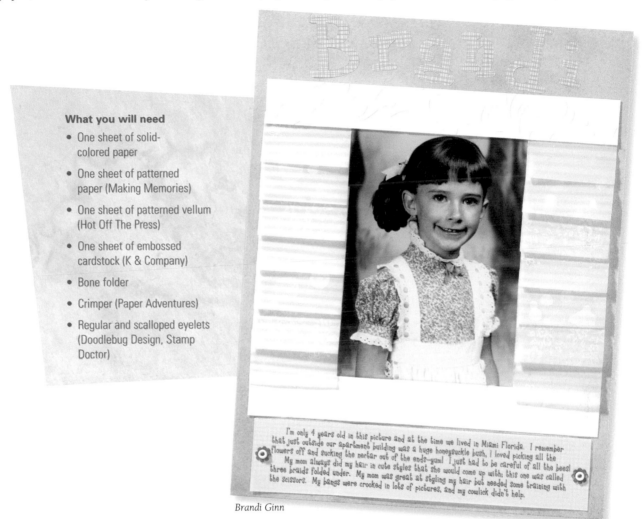

What you will need

- One sheet of solid-colored paper
- One sheet of patterned paper (Making Memories)
- One sheet of patterned vellum (Hot Off The Press)
- One sheet of embossed cardstock (K & Company)
- Bone folder
- Crimper (Paper Adventures)
- Regular and scalloped eyelets (Doodlebug Design, Stamp Doctor)

Brandi Ginn

1   Slice fourteen 2 x 2" patterned vellum squares; score at center with bone folder and fold in half lengthwise. Open folded strips; pass through crimper and refold strips carefully so as not to flatten out crimps. Layer horizontally on both sides of photo, with the folds pointing down, overlapping about one-fourth of an inch.

BARGELLOS
Like many contemporary paper techniques, "bargello" draws its inspiration from older crafts. Bargello was originally a needlework technique in which rows of color were used to create geometric shapes. Quilters and paper crafters then adapted it. Here, strips of paper are cut and folded to make abstract, yet traditional motifs—a perfect technique for the scrapbook page.

Erikia Ghumm

Layer a spectacular bargello background

Mix and match a variety of patterned papers for a stunning quilted background design. Experiment with the placement of the folded bargello strips and softer paper colors for an entirely different look. Follow the steps on pages 41 and 42 to create the bargello effect shown here. Double mat photo, leaving enough room on first mat for journaling. Freehand draw title letters. Outline letters in pen, silhouette crop, and mount on page with self-adhesive foam spacers.

What you will need

- Five to seven sheets of complementary-colored patterned papers (Hot Off The Press, Provo Craft, Scrapbook Wizard, Scrappin' Dreams)

- Bone folder

- Self-adhesive foam spacers

1 Cut numerous 1½" wide strips from a variety of complementary-colored patterned papers. The number of strips needed will vary depending on the size of your page and detail of the design.

2 With a bone folder and a metal straightedge ruler, score the backsides of all the strips lengthwise ¼" from the edge of each strip.

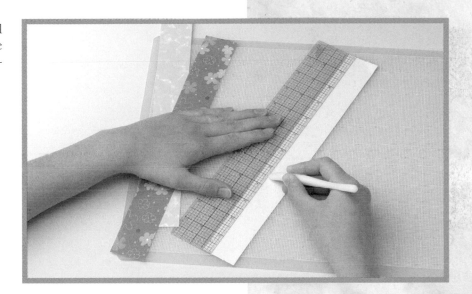

3 Fold the strips lengthwise on the scored lines, matching wrong sides together.

4 Use a pencil and a ruler to draw guidelines on solid-colored background paper where you want to begin adhering the folded strips. Alternate patterns and adhere folded strips diagonally starting in one corner and overlapping one over the other about ½", allowing the ends to hang off the page.

5 Continue alternating patterns and adhering strips diagonally to cover the second half of the background paper. When all diagonal strips are in place, mount vertical strips to hide diagonal strip ends and any pencil lines that may still be visible.

6 Turn the page over and use scissors to trim off any overlap, carefully cutting along the edges of the background paper.

Cut and fold a bargello mat

Layer folded strips of complementary-colored patterned papers into a textured mat perfect for highlighting a portrait. Rotate photo, mat or both in different angles for a varied effect. Start by slicing 1½" strips of patterned papers; score and fold lengthwise following steps on pages 41 and 42 to form folded strips that are ¾" wide. Layer onto an 8¼" square piece of paper, turn over and trim. Double mat bargello design. Quadruple mat portrait, mount on bargello mat design. Layer atop patterned background paper. Cut four ½" wide patterned paper strips; mat with solid-colored paper strips. Mount diagonally at each corner; turn page over and trim edges. Crop and journal matted title block; mount on page.

Kelly Angard

What you will need

- Four sheets of complementary-colored patterned papers (Colors by Design, Ever After, Frances Meyer, Karen Foster)
- Two sheets of coordinating, solid-colored papers
- Bone folder

IRISES

Popular in Holland, this paper technique mimics the iris diaphragm—or metal blades—that form the aperture opening of a camera lens. Cut and folded strips of paper softly overlap each other while leaving an opening in the center through which precious photos are revealed. The technique is created on the back of your scrapbook page, providing a creative surprise when you are finished and you turn your page over to reveal a magnificent photo frame!

Pennie Stutzman,
Pattern Margie Cotter

Craft elegant oval iris frames

The surprising art of iris folding results in gorgeous photo frames. We provide patterns for oval and rectangular iris frames, but you can easily create your own pattern by using a different template shape and drawing your own placement lines. Follow the steps on pages 45 and 46 to create the oval frames shown here on a 12 x 12" page. Print title and journaling on vellum. Frame title with additional strips of folded, patterned paper.

What you will need

- Four to six complementary-colored sheets of patterned papers (Hot Off The Press, Karen Foster, Colorbök)

- One sheet of cardstock for background

- Pattern on page 124

- Removable artist tape

- Bone folder

1 Cut twenty-five 2 x 6" strips from patterned papers for the large oval iris frame. Cut sixteen 2 x 6" strips for the small oval iris frame.

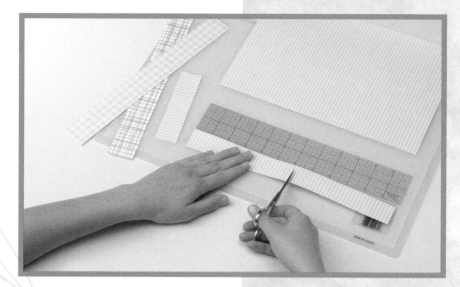

2 Use a bone folder to score strips in half lengthwise, then use bone folder to fold strips with wrong sides facing together.

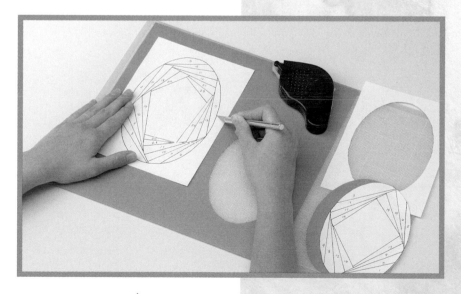

3 Photocopy and size patterns to fit scrapbook page. Position patterns on the front of your page where you want the oval frame openings to be; hold in place with removable artist tape, if desired. Use a craft knife to cut out the patterns' outer oval shapes only (don't cut on any of the pattern's interior placement lines; you'll need them for step 5). Or, use a graduated oval template or shape cutter that is the same size as your pattern to cut openings on scrapbook page.

4 Place pattern pieces face down over cut opening on the front of the page, centering so that the patterns' numbers and placement guidelines show on the back side of the page; adhere with removable artist tape.

5 You will work from the patterns' outer edges inward to adhere folded strips of paper in numerical order following pattern numbers. Place the folded edges inward toward the center of the pattern, overlapping strips as you go, staying true to the patterns' placement guidelines.

6 Continue adhering strips until the patterns are covered. Flip the page over and carefully remove the pattern so as not to tear page. Slip photos behind the patterned paper iris openings and mount in place.

Make a rectangular iris frame variation

The rectangular iris frame works great for horizontal photos. With either oval or rectangular frames, you can make the photo opening larger by not adding the last row of folded paper strips. Start with sixteen 2 x 7½" patterned paper strips. Then follow steps 2 through 5 on pages 45 and 46 to make the iris folded frame using pattern on page 124. Slip photo behind iris frame; mount in place on back of page. Cut title letters from patterned paper using template. Print journaling on vellum; mount on page with eyelets.

Pennie Stutzman, Pattern Margie Cotter

What you will need
- Patterned papers (Magenta, Provo Craft)
- Pattern on page 124
- Bone folder
- Lettering template (Cut-It-Up)
- Vellum
- Eyelets (Impress Rubber Stamps)

PLEATS

Like the freshly pressed dust ruffle over a box spring mattress, pleated photo mats and frames lend a smart, crisp look to your pages. The key to successful pleating, another paper craft adapted from sewing, is precise cutting and folding. Corners are then nipped and tucked by "mitering" them with a metal straightedge ruler and craft knife. Use pinch pleats for a soft, feminine look or try box pleats for a more rugged, masculine feel.

*Lynn Morgan for
Anna Griffin, Inc.*

Combine box and pinch pleats for elegance

Add an elegant touch to your page by folding patterned papers into pleated frames. Paper may be pleated along one edge or diagonally, but pleating always entails folding in opposite directions at marked intervals. Follow the steps on the following pages to create the box pleat and pinch pleat frames. Mat photo on patterned paper framed with silhouette cropped and matted ribbon design. Mount with self-adhesive foam spacers. Silhouette crop roses to adorn the frame's corners. Mat again on green patterned papers. Print title journaling on vellum; layer over printed title strip. Mount on paper cut and folded to look like ribbon.

What you will need

- Four sheets of coordinating patterned papers (Anna Griffin)
- Title strip (Anna Griffin)
- Bone folder
- 45° triangle (optional)
- Double-sided adhesive
- Self-adhesive foam spacers

1 *BOX PLEAT* Using a pencil and straightedge ruler, draw parallel lines alternating at 1" and ⅜" intervals across the back of patterned paper. Score lines with a bone folder and metal straightedge ruler.

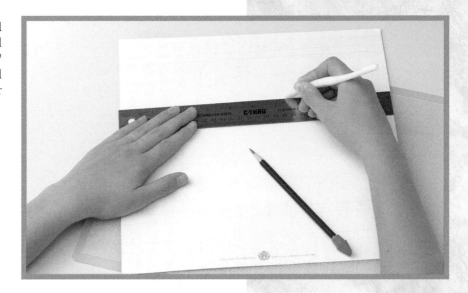

2 Start at one edge of the paper. Work your way across the paper pulling, pinching and pleating on scored lines, folding the ⅜" scores toward each other, alternating from front and back sides, until all folds are completed.

3 Cut pleats into ½" strips by holding all pleats down flat with a metal straightedge ruler on top of folded paper. Using a craft knife, slice down upon the folds, not up (see step 6 on page 126). Adhere double-sided adhesive across back of strips to hold pleats in place.

4 "Miter" corners with a metal straightedge ruler and craft knife, cutting at a 45° angle (use a 45° triangle if you have one), resulting in a clean, angled corner where border strips meet at page corners. Adhere pleated paper strips around page's outer edge. See steps 5 and 6 on page 126 for pinch pleat instructions to make the second row of pleats.

Torrey Miller; Photo Leslie Aldridge

What you will need

- Two sheets of coordinating patterned papers (Karen Foster, Scrap Ease)

- Two sheets of coordinating, solid-colored papers

- Bone folder

- Self-adhesive foam spacers

Create a raised box pleat variation

Add visual interest and dimension to a folded box pleat frame by layering patterned paper strips before folding and applying self-adhesive foam spacers to form peaks and valleys. Double mat photo and mount on matted background paper. Follow the steps on page 126 to create raised box pleat.

3

FOLDING & CUTTING

Think back to those childhood days when you made paper doll chains and snowflakes. Folding paper first and then cutting it provides a completely different spectrum of design possibilities than simply cutting paper or cutting and then folding it. In this section you will learn to:

- *Create paper chains, borders and frames using patterns or templates*
- *Embellish paper chains with stickers*
- *Fold and cut a multi-window "kirigami" frame*
- *Use decorative rulers and punches to create folded frames*
- *Transform a simple napkin fold into a poinsettia and snowflake*
- *Use a lettering template to create a personalized cut-out frame*

A few simple folds and some creative cuts will provide you with an endless supply of unique embellishments for your pages, no matter what their theme.

PAPER CHAINS

Remember when you opened your first chain of paper dolls? Like magic, the paper unfurled to reveal a line of little figures all linked together and holding hands. Experience the same sense of wonder by customizing paper chains to fit your scrapbook page themes for one-of-a-kind photo frames and page borders. With paper chains, your creative options are limitless.

Jodi Amidei

Fold and cut a paper chain

A folded and cut paper chain can serve not only as a border design, but also as the perfect resting-place for title letters. Experiment with any freehand-drawn shape or template shape to make quick-and-easy paper chains to match your page theme. Follow the steps on page 53 to craft the mitten paper chain shown here. Embellish mittens with pen details, snowflake punch and yarn or felt. Double mat photos; layer on page. Tear patterned paper; layer over matted background paper at bottom of page. Mount large mitten chain over torn paper for border. Stamp title letters on small mitten paper chain; mount across top of pages.

What you will need

- One sheet of patterned paper (Westrim)

- Three to four sheets of coordinating, solid-colored papers

- Patterns on page 124

- Small snowflake punch

- Letter stamps (Plaid Enterprises)

- Yarn (Lion Brand Yarn)

- Felt

1 Photocopy and size mitten patterns; cut out patterns. Fold paper—that is the same length as your page width—accordion style, making sure pattern fits the width of the folds.

2 Trace patterns onto folded paper, placing patterns' fold marks on the papers' folds.

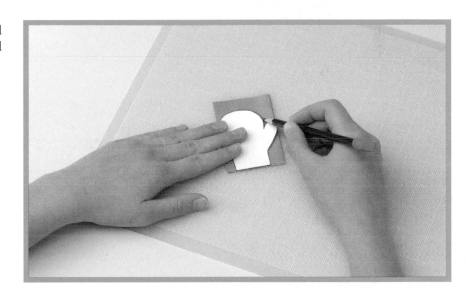

3 Cut out traced shape, being careful not to cut on the folds. Open the resulting paper chains and embellish as desired.

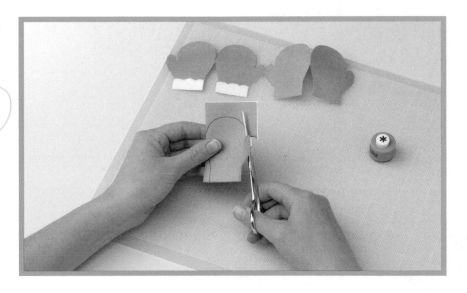

Lorna Christensen

Create a customized paper chain frame

It is easy to make a thematic paper chain by freehand drawing your design or tracing template shapes—joined by fold lines—onto theme papers. The freehand-drawn paper chain shown here is made up of snowman, snowflake and igloo shapes, and cut from embellished patterned papers. Follow the steps on page 55 to make the seasonal paper chain. Mat large photo; mount paper chain pieces around photo. Add pen detail to paper chain. Circle cut photos; mount on page and add pen detail around photos. Cut snowman shape from template; adhere title sticker letters. Mount second paper chain border along bottom of page.

What you will need

• Two sheets of coordinating patterned papers (Me & My Big Ideas)

• One sheet of coordinating solid paper

• Pattern on page 124

• Snowflake stickers (Mrs. Grossman's)

• Sticker letters (Creative Memories)

1 Embellish dot patterned paper strip with snowflake stickers for page border.

2 Fold both patterned papers in half lengthwise, with right sides facing in. Photocopy and size pattern twice—once for page border and again, smaller, for photo frame. Trace patterns onto embellished and patterned papers, making sure to connect the three designs together as shown.

3 Cut out around outer edges of design with scissors. Unfold paper chains and mount on page and around matted photo.

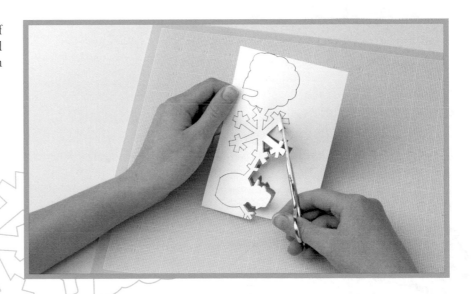

KIRIGAMI

The term "kirigami" comes from the Japanese words "kiri" and "kami" which mean "cut" and "paper" respectively. It is a traditional craft in which paper is folded and cut into decorative objects and designs. Kirigami is a versatile technique that can be used to give scrapbook pages a multicultural feel. Many traditional kirigami motifs are inspired by nature and can be adapted to fit themes ranging from romance to Christmas.

Ann Kitayama

Fold and cut kirigami windows

Create windows for photos to peek through with a simple fold-and-cut technique. Choose a template shape, or create one of your own that works with the theme of your photos. Follow the steps on page 57 to create the window pattern shown here. Crop photos to fit behind selected openings; mount to backside of windows. Layer and mount over solid-colored background paper. Complete page with title and journaling.

What you will need

- One sheet of patterned paper (Rocky Mountain Scrapbook Company)

- Pattern on page 124

- One sheet of coordinating, solid-colored paper

1 Four fold an 8½ x 11" sheet of patterned paper lengthwise at 2⅛" intervals (see page 126 for fold instructions).

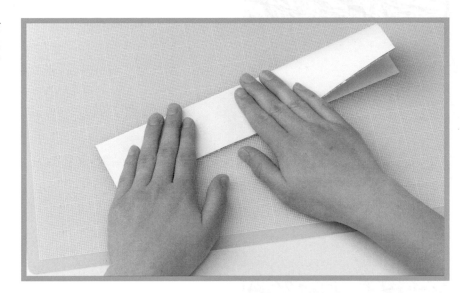

2 Photocopy and size pattern. Trace pattern or template shape of choice onto folded paper. Trace partial shapes over the folds of paper as shown in illustration on page 126 to create the all-over background pattern.

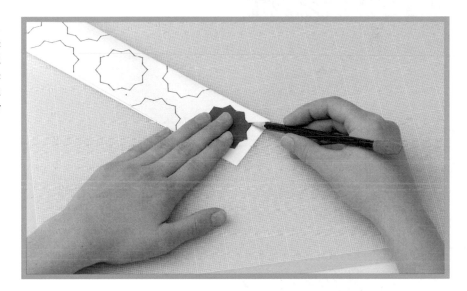

3 Cut out all traced lines with a craft knife and scissors. When all cuts are completed, open the folded paper and flatten the folds with a spoon (see page 14 for tips) or slightly warm iron (no steam or water!), if needed.

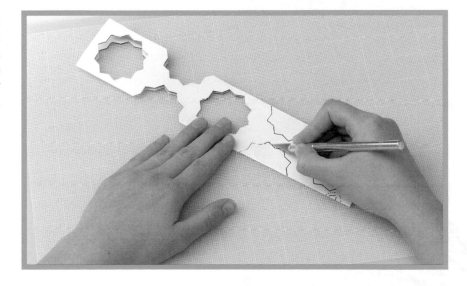

Punch a thematic kirigami frame

Highlight a beautiful holiday portrait with a paper-cut and punched kirigami frame. Alternatively, create your own theme frame with a different punch and vary the frame's inner edge with a different decorative ruler or with decorative scissors. Follow the steps on the next page to create the frame. Adhere photo behind frame. Mat framed photo on patterned paper; mount on page. Print title and journaling; cut to size and trim using decorative ruler. Attach vellum to page with eyelets. Mat smaller photo; mount on page over vellum. Cut two ⅛" strips of paper; mount on left side of page for accent.

Pamela Frye; Photo Jennifer Benedict

What you will need

- One sheet of patterned paper (Sandylion)

- Three sheets of coordinating, solid-colored papers

- Decorative border ruler (Cut-It-Up)

- Vellum (Karen Foster)

- Small tree punch (EK Success)

- Eyelets (Impress Rubber Stamps)

1 Double-fold a sheet of paper to be used as photo frame (see page 126 for illustrations for page 60 to create folds). Use a metal straight-edge ruler to draw two guidelines—one parallel and one perpendicular to the folds—to mark the opening of the frame. Trace decorative ruler design just inside drawn guidelines.

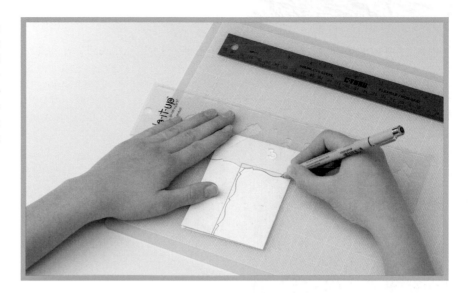

2 Draw punch placement guidelines at ¾" intervals around outer edges of folded paper, using a ruler and a pencil. Punch small trees atop the evenly spaced guidelines.

3 Cut the decorative lines to form the frame's opening with scissors. Unfold and flatten the folds' creases (see page 14).

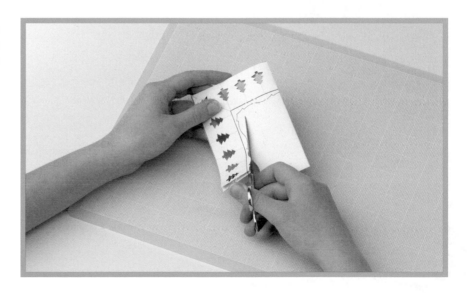

Fold and cut a kirigami heart frame

Enhance a treasured photograph with an elegant, symmetrical border-cut frame accented by hearts. Try making your unique version by freehand drawing or tracing cut lines with decorative rulers, adding a thematic shape for accent. First, cut a 4⅝" W x 5⅛" T window opening in an 8½ x 11" sheet of patterned paper, centered and 2" from upper edge of paper. Slip the photo behind window, center and adhere. Follow the instructions below (see page 126 for folding illustrations) to create the double-folded and cut suede paper frame. Mount over patterned paper. Cut title block, mat with suede paper trimmed with decorative ruler and scissors; adhere. Pen title and date.

Ann Kitayama

What you will need

- Two different sheets of monochromatic-colored patterned papers (Handmade Paper)

- Suede paper (Wintech)

- Pattern on page 125

- Decorative ruler (Westrim Crafts)

1 Photocopy and size the pattern on page 125 to fit photo or page size. Double-fold suede paper following instructions on page 126, folding with right sides together. Transfer pattern to paper (see page 13), matching up fold lines. Cut on lines with scissors. Unfold and flatten creases (see page 14).

Napkin-fold and cut kirigami poinsettias

Take the art of kirigami to an exciting level with napkin-folded flowers cut from delicate mulberry paper. Once you master the napkin fold, experiment with your own freehand-drawn patterns for unique kirigami embellishments. Follow the steps on the next page to create the poinsettia flowers and leaves in sizes that fit your page. Mount finished flowers and leaves over patterned background paper. Punch small circles for flower centers and adhere. Double mat photo. Cut title and journaling block; mat on solid-colored paper. Pen title and journaling.

Nick & St. Nick

This was the first year we couldn't get any of the kids to sit on Santa's lap. Instead we took their pictures with the St. Nick who sits on our church pew. 2001

Sharon Moore

What you will need

- One sheet of patterned paper (Bo-Bunny Press)
- One sheet each of red and green mulberry paper (Bazzill Basics)
- Two sheets of coordinating, solid-colored papers
- Poinsettia and leaf patterns on page 125
- 36° triangle pattern on page 125
- ¼" round hand punch

1 For the red poinsettia petals, begin with an 8½" square sheet of red mulberry paper. Fold the paper squares into a napkin fold (see page 126 for folding illustrations).

2 Photocopy and size flower petal pattern. Place cut pattern on folded paper, matching up the pattern's fold lines. Trace around the pattern's edges with a pencil.

3 Cut along the traced lines and unfold the poinsettia. Flatten out the fold creases (see page 14). Repeat the above steps to make the green poinsettia leaves.

Create symmetrical kirigami snowflakes

Symmetrical paper-cut designs, made from a napkin-folded paper pattern, dangle on a festive, winter theme page. Make the two snowflakes shown here using our patterns or draw and use your own snowflake pattern. Follow the steps below to create either snowflake. Mount snowflakes on solid-colored cardstock squares; chalk edges before matting. Double mat photos; mount on patterned background paper matted with solid-colored paper. Print title and journaling; cut to size and mat. Attach eyelets to title, journaling and snowflake blocks. Tie together with embroidery floss.

What you will need

- One sheet of patterned paper (Scrap Ease)

- Three to four sheets of coordinating, solid-colored papers (Bazzill Basics, Doodlebug Design, Robin's Nest)

- Patterns on page 125

- Eyelets (Doodlebug Design)

- Embroidery Floss (DMC)

- Chalk (Craf-T Products)

Sharon Moore

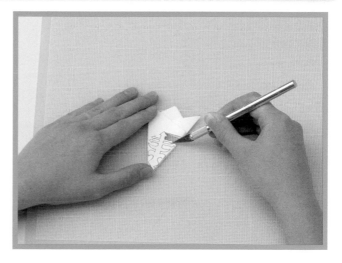

1 For the larger snowflake, begin with a 4" square of thin white paper. Note: It may be difficult to find acid-free white paper thin enough for kirigami. Consider using the white back side of a solid-colored or patterned paper. Fold paper into a napkin fold (see page 126 for folding illustrations). Photocopy and size snowflake patterns; cut out. Trace around pattern edges with pencil. Cut detailed design with a craft knife. Unfold and flatten out fold creases (see page 14).

Personalize a kirigami design

Incorporate a name, monogram or title into a symmetrical, personalized paper-cut design that can also serve as a frame for a photo. Use our pattern or create your own with template letters. Simply ensure that the first letter reaches both upper and lower edges of the folded paper triangle. Use upper- or lowercase letters; however, all letters must touch the lower fold of the triangle. Follow the steps below to cut the word "pals" into a symmetrical design. Cut word from two colors of paper; trim one word in second color. Layer over one section to highlight word. Mount photo at center of patterned paper; layer paper-cut design over photo and adhere. Fold and cut a freehand border design; mount around outside edges of background paper. Cut and pen title square.

What you will need

- Four sheets of complementary-colored patterned papers (Frances Meyer, Hot Off The Press)

- One sheet of coordinating, solid-colored paper

- Pattern on page 125

Pamela Frye; Photos Cristana Campbell

1 Transfer pattern to folded paper (see page 126 for folding illustrations). Cut outer edges of lettering with scissors, making certain not to cut through fold lines. Use a craft knife to cut out details at the center of letters.

4

LAYERING

Remember cutting and pasting images with wild abandon as a child,
without even knowing you were creating your first collage? Layering involves
adhering paper cutouts onto a page to create a picture or pattern.
Pre-existing paper patterns, photos and memorabilia are cut out and
reassembled to create a visual display whose sum is greater than
the total of its parts. In this chapter, you will discover how to:

• *Create "paper tole" using patterned papers*

• *Emboss and curl die cuts to give them a three-dimensional look*

• *Create Victorian-style pages using patterned paper collage*

• *Make an assemblage of complementary page elements*

• *Silhouette-crop photos and other design elements*

• *Tear paper to create an artistic montage*

These easy paper techniques will add yet another "layer" of creative
dimension to your scrapbook page design skills.

PAPER TOLE

Derived from the art of decoupage, "paper tole" involves shaping and layering several copies of an individual design element over a base print to create a three-dimensional effect. Paper tole provides the perfect way to highlight a favorite paper pattern or die cut in your album while accenting your photos.

What you will need

- Three duplicate sheets of patterned paper (Paper Adventures)
- One sheet of coordinating patterned paper (All My Memories) for mats
- Two sheets of coordinating, solid-colored papers
- One sheet of vellum (DMD Industries)
- Eyelets (Doodlebug Design)
- Flat sheet of craft foam
- Embossing stylus
- Bone folder
- ⅛" thick self-adhesive foam spacers

Kelly Angard

Paper tole with patterned paper

Turn flat images cut from patterned paper into fabulously layered, three-dimensional designs with a simple cut here and a few curls there. This technique works well with any patterned paper that has medium to large design elements. For this simple variation of our cover page, mat one sheet of trimmed, 12 x 12" patterned paper. Follow the steps on the next page to create paper tole elements; set elements aside. Add title and journaling to vellum, hand color and attach to page with eyelets along right border. Mat photos and arrange on page as shown. Mount paper tole elements atop their duplicate image on background paper, allowing some to overlap onto photos and title block.

1 Silhouette crop some randomly chosen design elements from the second and third sheets of patterned paper. Cut enough pieces to have two each of selected elements. Then, cut one each of the silhouette cropped elements into segments following natural cutting lines. You will have one whole butterfly and one pieced butterfly for each design element.

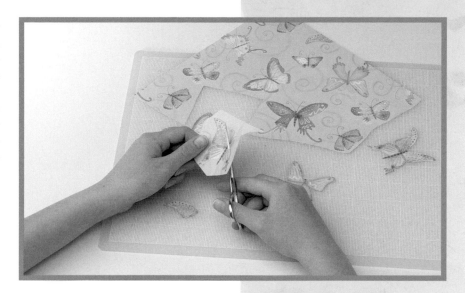

2 Lay each piece right-side-down on a soft surface such as a sheet of craft foam. Gently shape and curl each piece using a shaping tool such as an embossing stylus or bone folder. Repeat this step on all cropped and cut pieces

3 Then use the rounded tip of a bone folder to rub the butterflies and cut pieces in a circular motion to make the cut pieces curl. Rubbing too much can crumple the paper. Repeat this step on all cropped and cut pieces. Steps continue on page 126.

Curl die cuts for depth

Here's another quick recipe for paper tole dimension: Cut apart printed die cuts or "punch outs," curl each piece and layer over duplicate die cuts with self-adhesive foam spacers. First, follow the steps on the facing page to create the layered elements. Mat photos with paper and printed frame. Layer photos and dimensional die cuts on a solid background. For the window box, layer two identical pieces cut from a duplicate printed frame. Adhere letter stickers for title.

Lorna Christensen

What you will need

- One sheet each of coordinating plaid (Doodlebug Design) and gingham (Making Memories) patterned paper

- Two to three duplicate die cuts: frame (My Mind's Eye), flowers (Imaginations, Inc.), jar/bug (Doodlebug Design) and doll/dress/hair (EK Success)

- Embossing stylus or rounded bone folder

- Sheet of craft foam

- Self-adhesive foam spacers

- Letter stickers (Provo Craft)

1 For each dimensional design, obtain two copies of the same printed die cut. Lay the first die cut aside for the base or lower layer. Cut apart the duplicate die cut into its logical parts. For example, cut leaves apart from flowers and then cut additional slits between petals.

2 Lay each piece right-side-down on a soft surface such as a sheet of craft foam. Gently shape and curl each piece using a shaping tool such as an embossing stylus or bone folder. See Steps 2 and 3 on page 67.

3 Using self-adhesive foam spacers, layer shaped pieces over the base die cut in the same relative position. If desired, use additional layers for even more depth. For example, layer the bug die cuts on the jar die cuts.

COLLAGE

In collage, individually cut or torn items are arranged artistically on a page. There are many variations of this technique. In a Victorian-style collage like the one shown below, preprinted shapes are cut from patterned paper and rearranged to create a new background design. In an assemblage, both flat and three-dimensional items are combined. In a montage, the primary design element is your photos. Any collage style results in a memorable scrapbook page.

What you will need

- Three to four sheets of coordinating patterned papers (Anna Griffin)

- One sheet of coordinating, solid-colored paper

- Oval shape cutter or template

- Preprinted title strip (Anna Griffin)

Kelly Angard; Photo MaryJo Regier

Silhouette designs from patterned paper

Simple silhouetting is all it takes to create custom collage backgrounds and page elements. This cutting and layering technique works particularly well when you want to rearrange the designs on trimmed, patterned paper to better suit your layout. To enhance this heritage photo, Victorian flowers were layered to form a wreath-like frame. To create the floral background, follow the steps on the facing page. Double mat the oval photo. Use self-adhesive foam spacers to layer photo in page center with additional floral embellishments. Cut out and mat title strip.

1 Select patterned papers with large design elements that enhance the colors, theme or time period of your photos. For the matted background, select solid or tone-on-tone coordinating papers.

2 Using small, sharp scissors, silhouette crop each design element from patterned papers. Silhouetting is less fatiguing when you move the paper in and out of the scissor blades rather than moving the blade around the shape.

3 Arrange the silhouetted designs on the matted background. When you are satisfied with the arrangement, adhere each piece in place.

Assemble a visual story

Although collage means literally "to glue," most of us think of collage as a combination of layered paper images. In "assemblage," the collage is accented with three-dimensional items. There are no rigid rules for these paper techniques, but it helps to start with a theme and choose colors and objects to enhance it. For scrapbooks, select smooth, flat objects whenever possible. This whimsical assemblage combines patterned paper, ribbon, sewn-on vintage buttons, stickers, elements cut from magazines and hand-tinted, vintage photos. Refer to the steps on the following page for instructions. Incorporate a title and journaling into your design.

Sarah Fishburn

What you will need

- Four to five sheets of complementary-colored, thematic patterned papers (Colors by Design, The Paper Co., Sandylion)

- Assorted thematic stickers (Frances Meyer, Paper House Productions, Pressed Petals, Wordsworth Memories)

- Foreign postage-stamp reproductions (Art Accents)

- Flowers and butterfly images cropped from magazines

- Gingham ribbon

- Vintage buttons

1 Select a theme for your assembled collage based on your photos. Gather papers, photos and design additions to fit the theme, colors and style.

2 Select the background paper. Arrange the photos and other elements for visual appeal until you are satisfied with the design. This is a creative process that can take as little or as much time as you wish.

3 Silhouette crop photos and other paper items. Layer and mount elements in desired positions.

Tear a collage

There is something therapeutic about tearing paper. Perhaps it takes away the stress of a day! In any case, a layered montage with torn elements creates a soft and casual feeling. The key is to start with a photo as the focal point. Then layer torn paper shapes and design elements to complement the photo. Refer to the instructions below to arrange this school-theme layout. Mat the printed caption with torn green paper. For depth, mount the tassel die cut with self-adhesive foam spacers.

What you will need

- Three to four sheets of school-theme patterned papers (Colorbök, Colors by Design)

- One white or cream-colored sheet of cardstock for background

- Color photocopy of page from old nursery-rhyme or school book

- Children's art and writing

- Tassel die cut (Deluxe Cuts)

- Self-adhesive foam spacers

Torrey Miller; Photo Heidi Finger

1 Begin with a sheet of neutral cardstock as the background. Choose papers and other elements to complement the focal photo, colors and theme. Randomly tear paper strips and shapes. Layer elements alongside photo on the background, overlapping edges. When you are satisfied with the arrangement, adhere all design elements. Then flip the page over and trim away any overlapping edges with scissors.

5

TEARING

Tearing paper offers a decorative "edge" that softens the look of a page.
Tearing also provides surprising and spontaneous results depending
upon: The paper's texture and thickness; the direction of the tear; the speed
with which you tear; and how you guide the paper with your hand.
Here you will learn to:

• *Use a pattern to piece together a torn-paper design*

• *Alternate positive- and negative-torn "space" to create a page border*

• *Design a free-form page embellishment*

• *Make a mosaic utilizing torn tiles of colored paper*

• *Create translucent vellum backgrounds and overlays*

• *Incorporate lettering into a torn scene*

• *Use beads to mimic water on torn vellum*

• *Gild the edges of torn mulberry paper*

The act of tearing paper is as satisfying as the gorgeous results that torn
paper provides. Try these techniques, and you won't be able to
rip yourself away from tearing paper!

TEARING SHAPES

Paper piecing, borders and other embellishments take on a whole new form when shapes are torn instead of cut. Designs can look rugged, soft or whimsical—perfect for outdoorsy or playful layouts. The beauty of this technique comes from its imperfections; don't be afraid of making mistakes. Each tear lends character to your page.

What you will need

- Five to six sheets of earth-toned (see colors in caption), solid-colored papers
- Pattern on page 125
- Removable artist's tape
- Embossing stylus or bone folder (optional)
- Yellow pressed flower
- Clear photo corners (Canson)

Linda Strauss

Tear out paper patterns

A paper pattern makes it easy to achieve the torn look without having to do it all freehand.
Coloring books and clip art make great patterns for tearing. For this pocket title page, start with a dark sage background. Tear (see tearing tips on pages 9 and 14) the top edge of a light sage square to resemble a mountain range; adhere to background along left, lower and right edges to form pocket. Refer to the steps on the facing page to create the moose. Mount travel postcard with clear photo corners. For the title, cut a 2" speckled sage strip and tear thin brown strips for letter parts. Write letters with black pen and insert travel memorabilia.

1 Photocopy and enlarge the moose pattern on page 125 to fit your layout design. Cut out each pattern piece and mark the front sides.

2 Use removable artist's tape to temporarily attach each pattern piece to the appropriate colored paper. If you don't have removable adhesive, place the front of each pattern piece on the back side of the appropriate colored paper and trace. Carefully tear out each piece along the pattern edges. If the paper does not tear easily, try scoring the tearing lines with an embossing stylus or bone folder.

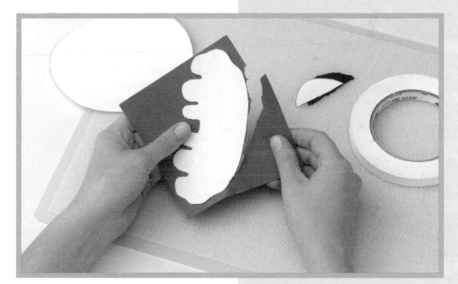

3 Arrange the moose pieces on the page background atop pocket. Mount in place. Add pressed flower to mouth. Use a black pen to outline the brown and white pieces.

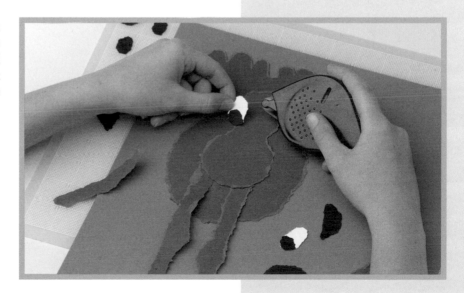

Contrast positive and negative shapes

Try this tearing technique with other designs such as stars, fish, flowers, leaves, letters or numbers. For the background, mount patterned tissue paper on white cardstock. Tear the left edge of a 7 x 12" brown rectangle and mount along right side of page. Mat photo with metallic gold. Print and tear out title and caption; outline with black pen. Follow the instructions below to tear out positive and negative brown hearts. Embellish layout with butterfly, flower and phrase torn from patterned tissue paper.

What you will need
- One sheet each of brown, white and metallic gold solid-colored papers
- Patterned tissue paper (source unknown)
- Gold metallic thread and sewing needle

A dream is a wish your heart makes

We're just a little BEHIND in our garden here. We had just moved to our new home and the yard didn't have a lawn yet. Mario escaped from the house to play in the water, June 1996.

Paradise

Linda Strauss

1 Start by tearing two 4" brown squares. Fold each square in half like a card. Tear out one half of a heart shape along the folded edge. If you'd rather not fold the paper, tear the heart shape directly into the paper leaving a seam at the lower edge, leaving the frame intact. Sew gold thread around the edges of one torn heart. Use both positive and negative torn shapes on page.

Shape natural elements

Use torn shapes to recreate objects from nature and add an impressionistic style to seasonal layouts. For the foldout summer page, tear and layer colored shapes to form clouds, cherry tree, hills and bees on a matted panel and attach to page with artist's tape. Accent with punched microdot red cherries. Layer matted photos, caption, title letters cut from template, triangles and squares on an aqua background. Tear leaves and cut and punch cherries for accent.

For the winter page, layer torn shapes to create snow, tree, rabbit and bird for border. Layer torn pieces for trees and snow atop light blue letters cut from template, trimming edges as needed. Accent matted photo with corner triangles embellished with birds torn from red and yellow paper. Draw details with black pen.

What you will need

- One sheet each of white, brown, lime green, dark green and yellow, solid-colored papers

- Two sheets each of red, aqua and light blue solid-colored paper

- Circle shape cutter or circle template

- Lettering templates (EK Success, Frances Meyer)

- Microdot and ⅜" circle punches

Alex Bishop

TEARING SCENES

Give your pages a change of scenery with torn-paper backgrounds made from tiny, tile-sized pieces of colored paper, strips of torn vellum and torn-paper shapes. For added impact, tear your page titles as well!

Shannon Taylor

Piece a mosaic backdrop

Round up the kids and put them to work. They will have a blast tearing normally off-limits scrapbook papers into small mosaic pieces. They can even help design the scene! Follow the steps on the facing page to create the background scene. Cut title letters from lettering template; detail with pen. Double mat photos, tearing edges of outer mats. Mat printed vellum caption with paper frame. Join caption to photo using eyelets and jute. Mount clovers on 2" paper square and slip into memorabilia pocket.

What you will need

- One sheet each of white, light blue, aqua, tan, brown, sage green and dark green solid-colored papers
- Gray chalk (Craf-T Products)
- Lettering template (EK Success)
- Vellum
- Eyelets
- Natural jute
- Pressed clovers
- 2 x 2" Memorabilia Pocket (3L)

1 Use a pencil to freehand draw outline for background scene. Keep the design simple with fairly large sections. If you find a design in a book or magazine that you want to use as a starting point, first turn it into a simple line drawing using tracing paper. Then transfer the drawing onto the layout.

2 Choose paper colors that best represent each element of the scene. Try patterned papers for added texture. For example, you might try "sand" patterned paper for a beach scene. Tear each paper color into small scraps no larger than ¾". Keep the colors separated and organized in plastic sandwich bags. Add dimension to the white pieces by shading the edges with gray chalk.

3 Glue the torn paper pieces in the appropriate sections of the scene, starting with the background elements and finishing with the foreground elements. Overlap edges as needed to cover the entire layout.

Create movement with torn vellum

If you remember the scene but forgot to take a picture, you can re-create it with multiple layers of colored and vellum paper. For this page, start with a sage background. Tear and layer vellum clouds and green mountains, shading mountains with black ink. Color-photocopy and enlarge printed pine trees, if desired. Silhouette-crop trees; mount with self-adhesive foam spacers. For the rocks, freehand tear and layer strips of colored vellum; top with silhouette-cropped photos. Use the computer font to make a pattern for the title letters. Adhere letters to the clip art frame.

Donna McMurry

What you will need

- One sheet each of sage and green solid-colored papers
- One sheet each of white and earth-toned colored vellum papers (The Paper Company)
- Black stamping ink
- Preprinted pine tree die cuts (The Beary Patch)
- Clip art frame (Carolee's Creations)
- Self-adhesive foam spacers
- Computer font (Microsoft)

Layer a vellum landscape

When torn, vellum has a soft white edge that adds subtle detail to this landscape scene. The natural elements further capture the beauty of the scenic photos. Begin with white cardstock as the page base and work from the top down. For the sky, layer white vellum over blue vellum. Tear and layer various shades of blue and green vellum for mountains, hills and journaling blocks. Mount photos and tuck in pressed ferns. Accent with pressed flowers.

What you will need

- One sheet of white cardstock for background

- One sheet each of white, light blue, dark blue, purple, green and goldenrod vellum papers (Strathmore)

- Vellum adhesive (3M)

- Pressed ferns and flowers (Nature's Pressed)

Linda Strauss

HAPPINESS IS IN THE JOURNEY

Here Joel and friends, Monica, Denis and Emily Fajardo, rent bikes to do some sightseeing in Jackson Hole, Wyoming.

1 Experiment with the placement of torn vellum landscape strips prior to adhering on background with vellum adhesive. When finished, turn page over and trim away any excess overlap with scissors.

Incorporate torn lettering

Blending these large title letters into the torn pond water prevents them from overwhelming this colorful fishing layout. For the background, layer tan on speckled blue paper. Crop and mat photos using corner rounder punch. Follow the steps on the next page to create pond water with title letters. Freehand cut pattern for green and tan grass. Mount grass beneath pond water title. Stamp and heat emboss fish using blue ink on light gray paper. Punch frogs and dragonflies, using white vellum for dragonfly wings. Draw details and write captions with white pen.

Debra McDonald

What you will need

- Two sheets each of light blue speckled patterned paper
- One sheet each of tan, light green, dark green, olive, aqua, blue and navy solid-colored paper
- One sheet of white vellum (DMD Industries)
- Corner rounder punch
- Small frog, dragonfly and egg punches (Carl, Family Treasures, McGill)
- Lettering template (C-Thru Ruler Co.)
- Bass stamp (Stampa Rosa)
- Blue stamping ink
- Clear embossing powder
- Self-adhesive foam spacers

1 First tear and layer paper to create the pond water that stretches across the bottom of the layout. Use the lettering template to lightly trace each letter in the desired position.

2 Use a craft knife to cut out each letter, through all torn paper layers. Use egg-shaped punch to punch holes out of the letters B and A. Mat letters with navy blue paper, leaving a thin border around the letters.

3 Mount letters so that they completely cover the cut-out openings.

Torn edge accents

Add polish to torn edges by accenting a title block with a vellum overlay and tiny beads to mimic water bubbles. Or line a page background with the rich look of torn mulberry gilded with metal flakes.

Chris Peters

What you will need

- Two sheets of duplicate patterned paper (Paper Adventures)

- One sheet each of light blue, dark blue and aqua solid-colored papers

- One sheet each of green and patterned vellum (Autumn Leaves)

- Lettering template (Scrap Pagerz)

- Diamond dust paper for letters (Paper Adventures)

- Vellum adhesive (3M)

- Liquid adhesive

- Clear seed beads (Westrim)

Imitate bubbly water

Torn vellum creates the perfect watery look, and now it's available in a patterned version that resembles water. The small seed beads mimic bubbles. Start with patterned bubble paper for the background. Crop and double mat photos and arrange as desired. Follow the steps on the facing page to create the title and caption. Write caption with blue pen.

1 Cut out the title letters using a lettering template. Mount letters on torn aqua square. Mat title with straight blue square and torn green vellum square. Use the water-patterned vellum for the title overlay. Freehand tear the upper edge of the vellum in a wavy pattern so it covers the lower two-thirds of the title block.

2 Mimic water bubbles by using tweezers and a liquid adhesive to mount clear seed beads along the upper edge of the vellum overlay. Allow to dry thoroughly.

3 Use torn strips of vellum adhesive to attach the vellum overlay to the title block at the sides and lower edges only. For the caption, create a similar vellum overlay for a 1½" matted blue strip.

Gild the edges of torn mulberry

Mulberry paper is the secret to beautiful feathery edges. One way to tear mulberry is to wet the line you want to tear, using water and small paintbrush. Then gently tear along the damp line. For straighter edges, try tearing dampened mulberry paper against the edge of a Deckle ruler as shown on page 14. For this wedding layout, tear multiple strips of colored mulberry and gild the edges as shown below. Layer the mulberry strips on a white background. Use blue paper and white mulberry to mat the photo and create the caption.

What you will need

- One sheet each of royal blue, peach, pink, light blue and white mulberry paper (PrintWorks)

- One sheet of coordinating, solid-colored paper

- Multicolored gold leaf flake (Amy's Magic)

- Gold leaf adhesive (Amy's Magic)

- Small paintbrush

- Tweezers

Our Moment in Time...
April 10, 1993

Kelly Angard

1 Carefully brush gold leaf adhesive on the feathery edges of each mulberry strip. Use tweezers to carefully apply the gold leaf to the wet areas. Keep your hands as dry as possible to prevent the gold leaf from sticking to them. Cover gilded paper strips with a clean sheet of paper and blot. Using a dry brush, dust away excess leaf and save for future use.

6

 Weaving

Paper weaving lends a rich textile look to your pages. And, like the fabrics that inspired them, woven paper designs vary in style from homespun to ethnic to elegant. Woven into this chapter are instructions on how to:

- *Make a tightly woven background out of straight paper strips*
- *Create a loose weave that makes the most of both positive and negative space*
- *Weave a random, wavy pattern or a randomly torn woven design*
- *Use a pattern to create a paper loom*
- *Cut a randomly curved loom*
- *Utilize a nested template to make a loom*
- *Create a woven, laced border with a Dutch feel*

Paper weaving is a much easier technique to accomplish than it may look. Master these simple techniques, and you will be ready to weave some scrapbook magic of your own.

WEAVING STRIPS
Paper strips are the basic materials used in paper weaving. Vary their thickness and spacing to create a variety of effects. Tight weaves look like a crisp placemat, whereas a loose weave gives an open, airy feeling. Wavy or torn strips are perfect for pages with rustic, outdoorsy themes.

Jodi Amidei

Craft a tightly woven mat

The under/over weave produces striking results when combined with solid and patterned papers. For this backdrop, cut 9½" long by ½" wide paper strips in the following quantities: 10 blue, 9 lavender, 18 patterned purple. Weave the strips following the steps on the next page. Double mat the weaving with purple, then blue paper. Mount diagonally on a plum background and trim corners. Arrange matted photos and caption. Use lettering template to cut out and mat title.

What you will need

- Two sheets of different purple patterned papers (Colorbök, Paper Adventures)

- Two sheets each of lavender and blue solid-colored papers

- One sheet of purple solid-colored paper

- Lettering template and computer font (Provo Craft)

1 Start with a ½" blue strip. With the blue strip on top, mount a ½" purple patterned strip perpendicular to the blue strip at the corner; adhere.

2 Mount a second purple patterned strip next the first, this time with the purple strip on top of the blue strip; adhere. Continue mounting purple strips across the width of the blue strip, alternating above and below.

3 Weave a ½" lavender strip under and over the patterned purple strips. Push snugly next to the first blue strip. Weave the next row over and under with a blue strip. Repeat this step until you have completed the weaving, alternating lavender and blue strips. When you have finished, trim the ends of each row if needed and use artist's tape to secure the strips in place on the backside of the weaving.

Weave a loose lattice

This variation of the under/over technique gives the illusion that the background color is actually woven into the design. The lattice works particularly well for this layout because the patterned strips reflect the colors of the sunset photo while the contrasting gray background tones down the overall effect. Begin with a black page. To weave the lattice, follow the steps on the facing page. Mat photo with black and mount on lattice. Freehand outline title on patterned paper using the template as a guide. Cut out title and mat with black. Write caption with black pen.

Nancy Korf

What you will need

- One sheet of sunset patterned paper (Wübie)
- One sheet of gray paper
- White pencil
- Lettering template (EK Success)

1 Start with an 11½" square of gray paper. Use a ruler and white pencil to mark the placement for the weaving strips, starting ⅝" in from the upper left corner. Make two "tick marks" ¼" apart for each strip. Allow ¾" spacing between each strip. Mark all four sides of the gray square in the same manner.

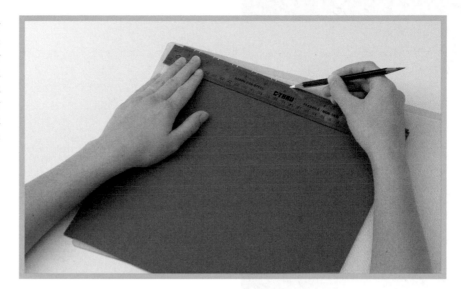

2 Cut 22 patterned strips ¼" wide by 11½" long. Place 11 strips vertically on the gray square, positioning them on the tick marks. Adhere the upper ends in place.

3 Weave the first horizontal strip over and under. Adhere the ends so they cover the tick marks. Weave the second horizontal strip under and over, securing the ends in place. Continue weaving until you have completed the lattice. When you have finished, adhere the lower ends of the vertical strips in place. Mat the entire lattice with a 12" black square.

Cut random wavy strips

Add a casual look to a loose under/over weave by using wavy, free-form strips in bright colors. Integrate the photos into the design by layering them beneath some of the strips. When you're pleased with the arrangement, mount the elements on a tan background. Write captions on vellum with blue pen. Highlight each letter with a light blue pen. Cut out each caption with wavy edges to mimic the weaving strips.

Pamela Frye; Photo Sandra Escobedo

What you will need

- One sheet each of tan, brown, orange and blue cardstock

- One sheet of white vellum (DMD Industries)

Tear colored vellum

Give the edges of your weaving a finished look by folding the ends to the backside of the background paper. The torn vellum strips further soften this basic over/under weave for a light, airy look. To create the woven background, follow the instructions below. Double mat both the weaving and the photos. Print, cut out and mat the caption. Fill the title letters with colored pencils. Punch ferns from colored vellum.

Jodi Amidei

What you will need

- One sheet each of rust, goldenrod, cream and light green vellum (Paper Adventures)

- One sheet each of rust, goldenrod and cream solid-colored papers (Club Scrap)

- *Agent Orange* font (downloaded from Internet)

- Colored pencils

- Fern leaf punch (The Punch Bunch)

1 Tear colored vellum strips approximately ¾" to 1" in width. Arrange eight vellum strips vertically on a cream background. Fold the ends over the top and bottom edges and secure on the back. Flip the page over and weave in the horizontal strips. Fold and secure the ends in the same manner.

WEAVING ON A LOOM

A loom provides a framework within which paper strips can be woven. You can make a loom by using a pattern, tracing the edges of a decorative ruler, or cutting along the grooves of a nested template. The loom provides a basic structure to your design that allows you to experiment with paper strips of varying shapes and widths.

Kelly Angard; Photos Helena Schwartz

Cut a symmetrical loom

This seemingly complex background is created from a symmetrical loom made by cutting slits in a folded sheet of paper. Simply follow the steps on the facing page to re-create the look. Triple-mat the photos. Cut the patterned title letters using the template. Mount each letter beneath a vellum rectangle and outline with black pen. Adhere letter stickers for the smaller words. Write the caption on a separate vellum rectangle using a letter sticker for the first letter. Weave ¼" aqua strips through vertical slits cut in both the title and caption.

What you will need

- One sheet of 12 x 12" purple solid-colored paper for loom
- One sheet each of yellow, aqua and orange solid-colored paper
- One sheet of patterned paper (Colors by Design)
- One sheet of translucent white vellum
- Pattern on page 125
- Removable artist tape
- Lettering template (Frances Meyer)
- Letter stickers (Provo Craft)

1 Photocopy and size the pattern to fit one-half of a 12 x 12" scrapbook page. Fold purple paper in half. Attach the pattern to the folded paper using removable artist's tape, taking care to match the fold lines. Secure both the pattern and paper to a cutting mat with removable artist tape or tape to paper and cut with scissors.

2 Use a metal straightedge ruler and craft knife to cut the pattern lines through all layers. Take care to start and stop the cuts according to the pattern. Remove the pattern and unfold the purple paper.

3 Cut yellow, aqua and orange strips of various widths. Loosely weave the strips into the purple loom. Start at the top and work your way down, alternating colors with each row. Secure the ends of each strip and trim away any excess.

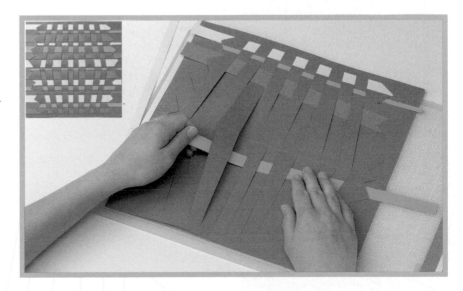

Try asymmetrical woven waves

Cutting wavy slits in a patterned background creates an asymmetrical loom that is woven with coordinating solid strips. Use our wavy line pattern or create your own lines with a decorative ruler. Follow the steps on the next page to weave the loom. Crop, mat and layer the photos with star die cuts. Use the wavy ruler you created in step 2 to cut and mat a banner strip for the title. Cut the title letters using the template. For the caption, mount white paper beneath a star die cut. Write the caption with blue pen.

Kelly Angard; Photos Cynthia Anning

What you will need

- Two duplicate sheets of patterned paper (Making Memories)

- Three sheets each of black and red solid-colored papers

- One sheet of white solid-colored paper

- Pattern on page 125

- Star die cuts (Ellison)

- Lettering template (The Crafter's Workshop)

1 Cut red, white and black strips in various widths ranging from ⅛" to ½".

2 Photocopy the wavy line pattern on page 125 and transfer to white cardstock to create a decorative ruler. Place the ruler edge about ½" from the top edge of the patterned paper and trace the wavy line with a pencil. Move the ruler down 1" and draw another wavy line. Repeat every inch down the paper until you reach the bottom. Carefully cut each wavy line with a craft knife, taking care not to cut through the left and right edges of the page. Repeat for a second loom.

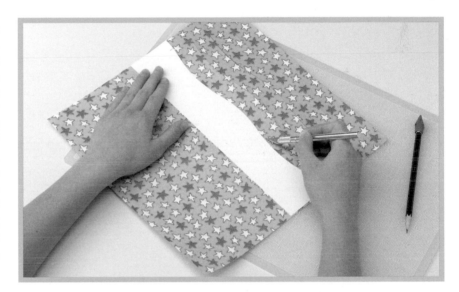

3 Randomly weave colored strips into the looms working from left to right. Secure the ends in place and trim excess. Double mat both weavings to complete the backgrounds.

Make a graduated template loom

A circle-cutting graduated template makes it easy to create a circular loom. The design gives a strong sense of movement to this superhero page. Try other shapes of graduated templates to make a varied loom. To re-create this look, mat the patterned background with navy paper. Mount a red rectangle in the page center. Create the circle weaving following the steps on the facing page. Mount the weaving as shown and trim the right side. Crop and mat the photos and write a caption. Adhere letter stickers for the title.

What you will need

- One sheet of patterned paper (Stamping Station)

- One sheet each of navy, blue, yellow, red and white solid-colored paper

- Coluzzle® Nested™ Circle Template (Provo Craft)

- Foam cutting mat

- Swivel cutting knife

- Letter stickers (Provo Craft)

Kelly Angard

1 Cut eighteen ¼" wide strips from solid-colored papers in quantities of: 6 red, 6 blue and 6 yellow.

2   Place the nested circle template over white paper on a foam cutting mat. Insert the swivel knife into a template-cutting channel and make the cut. Repeat until all template channels are cut. Remove the template and complete the cut on the outermost channel to allow the circle loom to fall away from the rectangular frame.

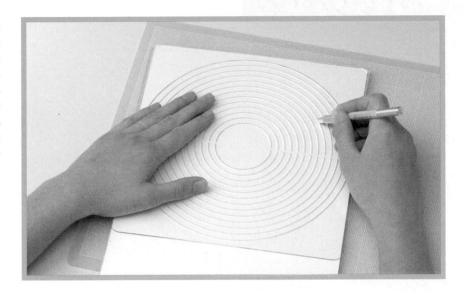

3   Weave four strips into the center of the loom to hold the loom together. Use a craft knife to complete the channel cuts, forming full circles.

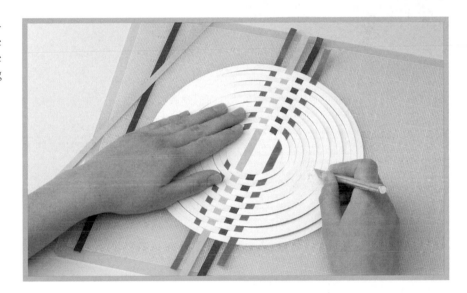

4   Weave remaining strips vertically into the loom, alternating colors as you go. Trim the end of each strip leaving a ⅛" overhang. Insert a ½" red strip horizontally through the center to cover the uncut center portion of the loom. Trim ends.

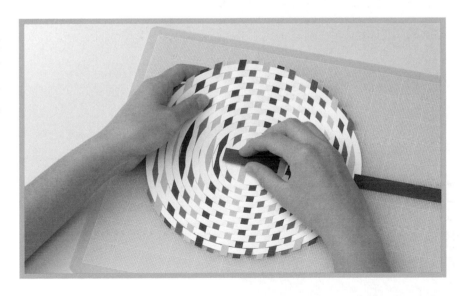

DUTCH-INSPIRED WEAVING

The laced weaving patterns on these pages look like the delicate embroidery of a Dutch girl's bonnet. Weaving thin strips of paper through cut slits in cardstock creates the traditional laced border and heart and flower motifs. These patterns give a finishing touch to baby, springtime or valentine layouts.

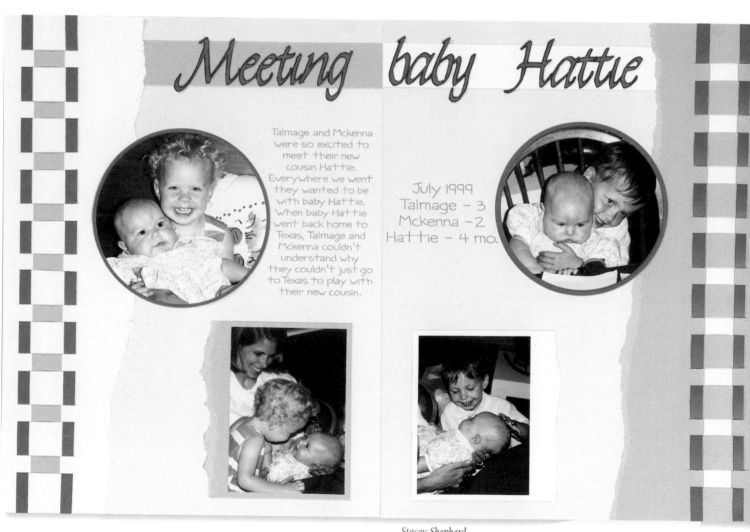

Stacey Shepherd

Lace a delicate border

Laced borders are the ideal choice if you like the woven look but want to save a little time. Start by printing a caption on one side of a pale sage background. Mount 1" blue and yellow strips across the top. Print and silhouette-crop title letters. Follow the steps on the facing page to lace the woven borders. Mount the borders as shown on the layout. Crop and mat photos, tearing mat edges as desired. Add journaling.

What you will need

- Three sheets of sage solid-colored paper

- One sheet each blue and teal solid-colored paper

- One sheet of yellow, mini corrugated paper (DMD Industries)

- Pattern on page 125

- Computer font (Provo Craft)

- Circle shape cutter or circle template

- Removable artist's tape (optional)

1 Tear the inside edges of each border strip so that the finished width is between 2" and 3". Starting ¼" from the left straight edge and ¾" from the top edge, use a pencil and clear ruler to lightly draw a horizontal cutting line 1¼" long on the back of the paper. Draw a second cutting line ⅜" below the first. Draw a third cutting line ¾" below the second. Continue drawing lines, alternating the spacing between ⅜" and ¾". If you prefer, photocopy the pattern on page 125 and secure it to the border strip using removable artist's tape and cut through pattern and paper on cutting lines.

2 Use a craft knife to cut through each penciled line. If you are using a pattern, cut the lines through both the pattern and the border strip.

3 Cut two ½" strips and four ¼" strips. Weave three strips into each border, one wide and two narrow.

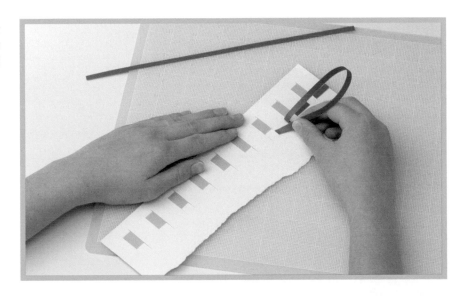

Laced hearts and flowers

These miniature weavings add form and texture without adding a lot of bulk. Once you understand the basic technique, you can easily create custom designs. To create the heart borders and flower accents, follow the steps on the next two pages. Start with a textured lavender background for the layout. Write the title with purple pen using the font as a pattern. Outline each letter with black pen. Mat and arrange all page elements.

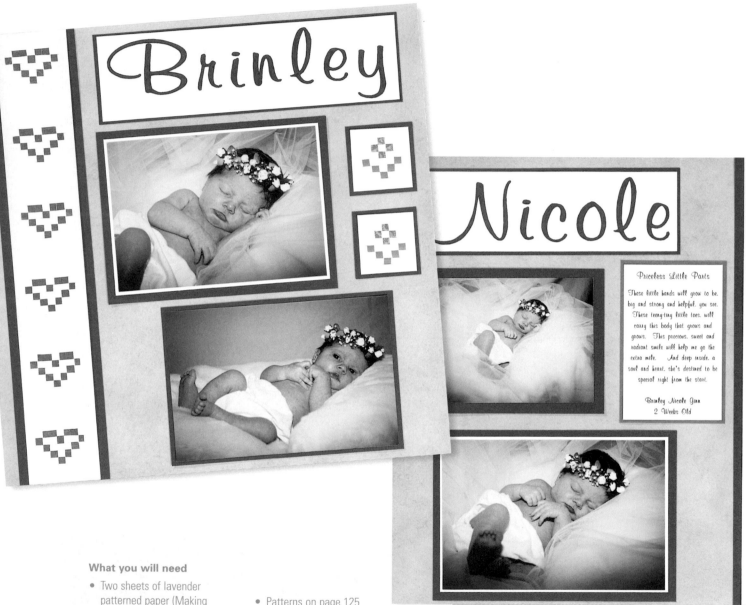

Brandi Ginn

What you will need

- Two sheets of lavender patterned paper (Making Memories)

- Two sheets of purple solid-colored paper

- One sheet each of white, red and green solid-colored paper

- One sheet of purple vellum paper (Paper Adventures)

- Patterns on page 125

- Computer font (downloaded from Internet)

- Poem from *The Scrapbooker's Best Friend, Volume II* (EK Success)

1 *HEARTS* For each heart border cut seven red strips ⅛" wide and 12" long. For easier lacing, use papers that are lighter weight than cardstock. For variety, you can also use paper quilling strips, satin ribbon or strips of fabric. To make the lacing easier, cut one end of each strip at an angle.

2 Photocopy and size the pattern to fit the page and place over a 2 x 12" white border strip. Use a metal straightedge ruler and craft knife to cut along the pattern lines, going through both the pattern and border strip. Remove the pattern. Using just the tip of the knife, slice through each cutting line again to help widen each slot so the paper will slide through more easily.

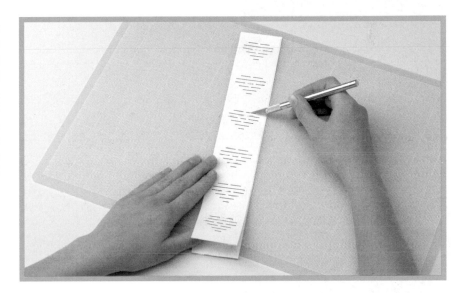

3 Starting at the lower left corner of the border, thread a strip through the back to the front and then down through the slot just above it. Working from the bottom up, continue lacing in and out all the way to the top of the border. Lace the remaining strips in the same manner, tucking each strip snugly against the previous one. Pull strips taut with each new weave, leaving a ¼" over-hang on the backside. If a paper strip tears while you are weaving, simply trim it on the back and insert a new strip so that the seam does not show. Follow steps 2 and 3 on the next page to complete the heart border.

1 *FLOWERS* For each flower, cut one red patterned strip and one green strip, each ⅛" wide and 12" long. Using the pattern on page 125, lace the design in a manner similar to steps 2 and 3 on the previous page. Work from left to right, weaving all the green strips; trim the ends on the backside. Then weave the red strips from left to right.

2 Turn the finished weaving over and trim excess extending beyond the edges of the white background.

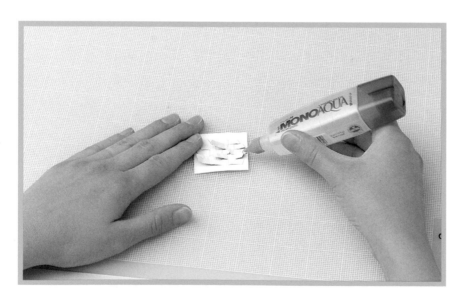

3 Use a liquid adhesive to lightly glue the ends of the laced strips in place. Mat each weaving to further secure the design.

7

QUILLING

Quilling is a craft in which thin strips of paper are coiled, shaped and adhered into and onto designs. The craft—which originated in Europe and spread to America during colonial times—got its name from the feather quills around which the paper was originally rolled. Nowadays special needles are available for use as quilling tools. The following pages will show you how to:

- *Make basic shapes out of quilling paper strips*
- *Apply just the right touch to skillfully shape coils*
- *Combine shapes to create freestyle designs*
- *Quill letters and numbers*
- *Add dimension to stamped or printed images*
- *Incorporate encapsulated quilling into your layouts*

Quilling is a relaxing and rewarding paper technique. While intricate designs do take time to create, there are also simpler quilling techniques for those with less patience. Learn how to quill, and you will become part of a beautiful paper craft tradition spanning many generations.

BASIC QUILLED SHAPES

With a squeeze here and a pinch there, coils of paper are transformed into beautiful shapes such as flower petals, teardrops, stars, holly leaves and tulips. The key to successful quilling is patience. With practice, you will learn how much tension is required to create each type of coil and how much pressure is necessary to alter its shape. The following quilling shapes are the most commonly used. They can be joined together in a multitude of ways to create new designs.

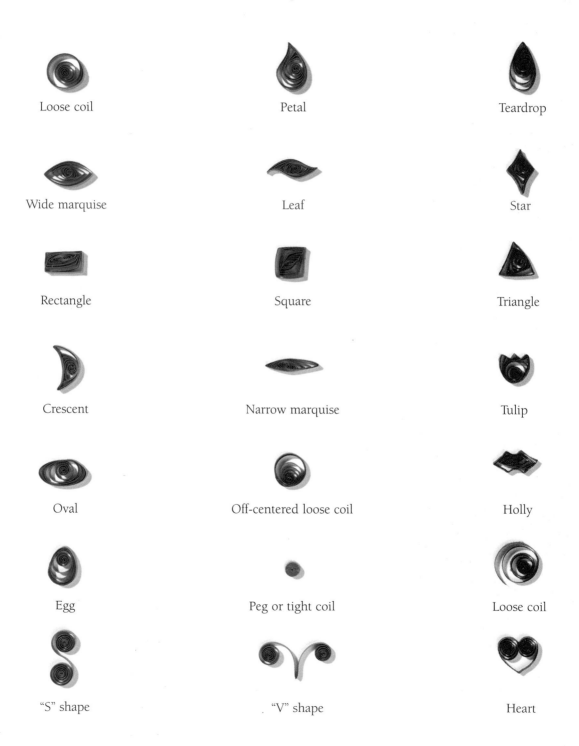

Loose coil

Petal

Teardrop

Wide marquise

Leaf

Star

Rectangle

Square

Triangle

Crescent

Narrow marquise

Tulip

Oval

Off-centered loose coil

Holly

Egg

Peg or tight coil

Loose coil

"S" shape

"V" shape

Heart

1 Most basic quilled shapes begin as a circle—coiled either loosely or tightly—and are then pinched into a more defined shape. To form a basic circle, insert one end of a strip of quilling paper into the tip of a slotted needle. Roll the handle of the tool with one hand as you let the paper coil between your thumb and fore finger of the other hand. You control how loosely or how tightly the coil is rolled.

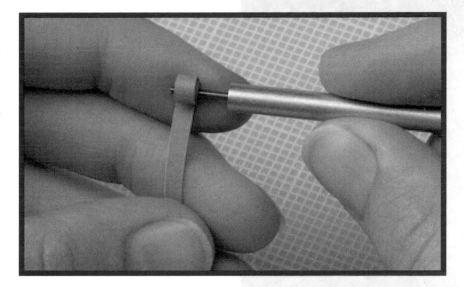

2 Once the coil is rolled, tear the end of the paper strip to provide a "seamless" seam for gluing. Apply a tiny drop of liquid adhesive to the inner side of the paper tail and press it against the roll. Allow quilled coil to dry.

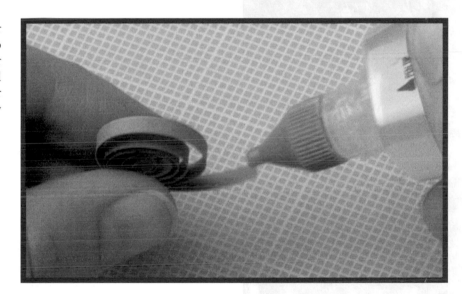

3 To create any of the shapes shown on the facing page, gently pinch the coiled circle between the thumb and forefingers of both hands, coaxing the circle into the desired shape. In the example shown, the circle is being pinched into a wide marquise shape.

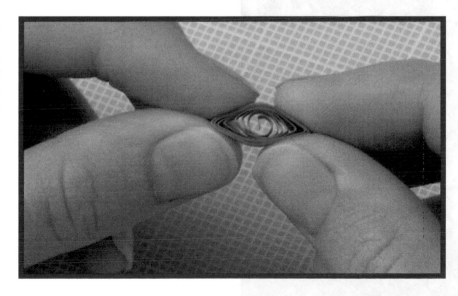

FREESTYLE QUILLING

Quilled shapes can be combined on your page to create elaborate designs. A circle and teardrops become a flower; elongated shapes such as the "S" are transformed into vines and tendrils. Try combining other shapes to create your own freestyle embellishments.

Ruth Mason

Design free-form floral accents

Learn to form basic quilling shapes and you will be off and running with this unique and striking paper technique. These floral arrangements create a dramatic frame for brightly colored summertime photos. Follow the steps on the facing page to create the quilled designs. Then crop and mat the photos using circle and oval cutters and a corner rounder punch. Trim selected mat edges with decorative scissors. Write captions on paper rectangles using a brown pen.

What you will need

- Two sheets of cream-colored cardstock
- One sheet each of yellow, green and pink solid-colored paper
- Assorted colors of $1/16"$ and $1/8"$ quilling papers (Lake City Craft)
- Small daisy, small oak leaf punches
- Jumbo grass clump punch (Nankong)
- Corner rounder punch
- Circle and oval shape cutters or templates
- Decorative scissors (Fiskars)

1 The floral corner accents are designed around a base of quilled tendrils. Create these tendrils using ⅛" green quilling paper, curving the strips and rolling the ends in loose coils. Mount the strips as shown in the areas in which you wish to create corner designs.

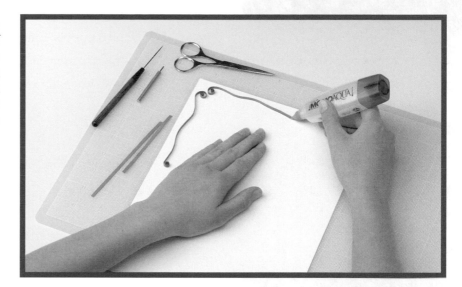

2 Quill the necessary shapes to create the floral design. The base tendrils are embellished with leaves and vines made with ⅛" paper coiled into heart shapes and "S" and "C" scrolls. Quill the larger colored flowers with ¹⁄₁₆" paper using tight coils for the centers and marquise shapes or loose, glued coils for the petals. Quill more petals of each color than you need so you can select the best for each flower. For the small daisies, curl the petals of punched daisies upward and glue tight coils in the centers. For the tiny orange flowers, fringe ⅛" orange strips and quill in a tight coil, pressing the fringe outward. Quill additional teardrop and marquise shapes to embellish the design.

3 Assemble the quilled shapes around the base tendrils, layering the flowers and leaves with punched oak leaves, trimmed strips for grass and punched grass clumps. Glue designs in place.

QUILLED LETTERS & NUMBERS

Looking for a unique page title accent? Try a quilled alphabet. As with other lettering techniques, your letters should be proportional to each other. Try mounting your titles on letter blocks and embellishing them with quilled flowers and other decorations.

Ruth Mason

Sculpt a quilled title

Quilled letters add the finishing touch to this delightful garden of spring flowers. Self-adhesive foam spacers make the upper title words stand out while protecting the delicate letters from being crushed. First crop and mat photos. For the title, freehand cut rectangles and punch squares. Adhere letter stickers and quill letters as shown on the facing page. Embellish title with punched daisies. Stamp and cut out orange butterflies, curving wings as in paper tole. Quill flowers and leaves, cut stems and background grass. Assemble and mount design with grass dies cuts and punched flowers.

What you will need
- Assorted solid-colored papers
- Assorted colors of $\frac{1}{16}$" and $\frac{1}{8}$" quilling papers (Lake City Craft)
- Corner rounder punches
- Circle punches: $\frac{1}{8}$" and $\frac{3}{16}$"
- $\frac{5}{8}$" square punch (All Night Media)
- Medium flower punch

1 Use the letter and number samples below to quill letters. Use graph paper to keep the size of the letters consistent. Lay each letter on graph paper and adjust the size as necessary to fit the desired grid.

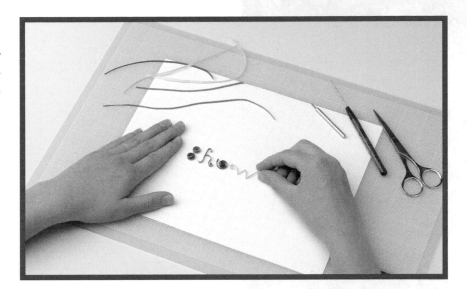

- Small daisy and mini sun and flower punches (Family Treasures, Fiskars)

- Letter stickers (Making Memories)

- Butterfly Stamps (All Night Media, Stampendous)

- Black stamping ink

- Grass border die cuts (source unknown)

- Self-adhesive foam spacers

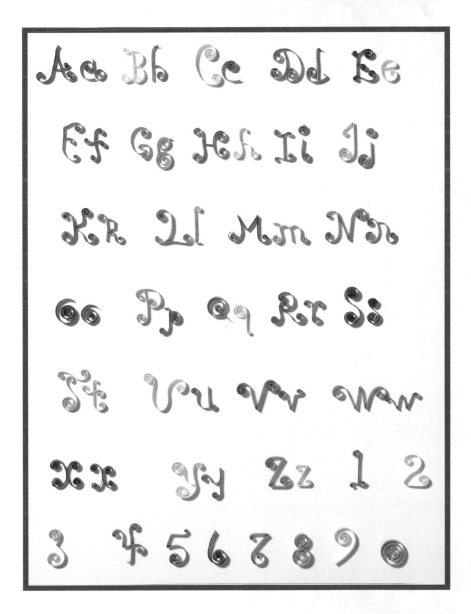

QUILLED IMAGE ACCENTS

Add dimension to rubber-stamped images, clip art and patterned paper with quilled accents that echo shapes in the printed designs. Flowers seem to come alive, balloons appear ready to float away, and gum balls look good enough to eat!

What you will need
- One sheet of patterned paper (Sonburn)
- One sheet each of green and white solid-colored paper
- Corner rounder punch
- Bulb stamps (Stampin' Up!)
- Black stamping ink
- Colored markers
- Assorted colors of 1/16" quilling

Jan Williams;
Photo MaryJo Regier

Embellish stamped images

Look no further than your stamping toolbox for quilling design ideas. There are thousands of stamp images available and most can be accented and enhanced with quilling. For the patterned paper background, mount a 1/4" evergreen strip along the top. Crop and double mat the photo using a corner rounder punch and a printed caption. Stamp, color, punch and mat each flower. Quill the floral designs as explained below.

1 Choose quilling paper to match the color of each flower. Quill loose coils, glue the end and place each coil on the stamped image to determine the appropriate size. Pinch each coil to fit the outline of the stamped image. For the leaves, quill larger loose coils, glue ends and pinch into marquise shapes. Freehand cut flat leaves. Glue design in place, layering as necessary and adding fringed accents.

Fill in a stencil shape

Like stamps, stencil designs lend themselves well to quilling, as does clip art. The background paper inspired the seahorse motif on this poolside page. Follow the instructions below to quill the design. Use an oval cutter to crop the oval photos and mats for the title and caption. Adhere sticker letters and write caption. Crop and mat rectangular photo using a corner rounder. Silhouette-crop remaining photo. Cut a partial page frame from two shades of solid cardstock. Layer elements on the patterned background.

Jan Williams

What you will need

- Two sheets of seahorse patterned paper (Paper Adventures)

- Two sheets of coordinating, solid-colored papers

- Oval shape cutter or oval template

- Gold glitter sticker letters (C-Thru Ruler Co.)

- Corner rounder punch

- Pattern from *The Big Book of Nature Stencil Designs* (Dover Publications)

- Blue, aqua and sage green ¹⁄₁₆" quilling papers (Lake City Craft)

1 Follow the directions on page 13 to transfer the seahorse pattern to the background paper. To make the seahorse, roll a tight aqua coil for the eye and loose coils for the remaining parts. Pinch the coils into squares, rectangles and other shapes to fit the pattern. For the seaweed, roll and pinch narrow marquise, leaf and teardrop shapes. Arrange the pieces to fit the pattern and glue in place.

Bring patterned paper to life

Look for designs in background papers that you can embellish with quilled shapes. Bright blue birds and fat balloons with spiral strings add both dimension and color to this picnic layout. Starting with a printed background design, select the elements that you want to embellish with quilled shapes. Roll and pinch the shapes to fit the objects and glue in place; add punched eyes to birds. Refer to the step below to roll a spiral. Crop the photos, mats and oval frame. Cut a slit in the background page along the lower edge of the design. Layer photos in page center, tucking lowest photo beneath slit in page. Write caption with blue pen.

Olivia celebrated her 1st birthday with a backyard picnic. The kids sure had fun watching the wacky clown!

Jan Williams

What you will need

- One sheet of patterned paper (Frances Meyer)

- One sheet of coordinating, solid-colored paper

- Blue, yellow, pink, purple, brown and black $1/16$" quilling papers (Lake City Craft)

- $1/16$" circle hand punch (Fiskars)

- Oval shape cutter or oval template

1   To make a spiral, wrap a quilling strip tightly around a sewing needle for small spirals or around a quilling needle for large spirals. Pull to loosen as necessary.

Encapsulate quilled designs

Plastic memorabilia holders protect quilled pieces and may also be utilized as an element in your page design. First quill the gum balls to fill the 3-D Keeper as shown on the facing page. Cut a circle in the blue background paper large enough for the 3-D Keeper and mount from the backside. Use the pattern on page 125 to cut out the gum-ball machine from red and black paper. Crop and mat photo and printed title. Embellish with additional quilled gum balls.

What you will need

- One sheet of patterned paper (Hot Off The Press)

- One sheet each of blue, red, black and white solid-colored papers

- Circle 3-D Keeper™ (C-Thru Ruler Co.)

- Assorted colors of ⅛" quilling paper (Lake City Craft)

- Pattern on page 125

Jan Williams;
Photo MaryJo Regier

1 For gum balls, use a 6" length of ⅛" quilling paper. Roll strips into loose coils about ⁵⁄₁₆" in diameter and glue ends. Place coils in circle 3-D Keeper and glue in place. Replace the plastic lid.

Quilled present

Try this design for a birthday or holiday page. Using 6" lengths of ⅛" quilling paper, roll loose coils and pinch into square shapes. Fill square 3-D Keeper with coils to create gift box design. Add punched bows and embellish with loosely rolled coils and teardrops rolled from 1/16" paper.

Jan Williams

Quilled heart

Quilled hearts arranged in a heart shape are an easy embellishment for any romantic layout. Using 4" lengths of ⅛" quilling paper, roll "S" coils with 1" at one end and 3" at the other. Glue two "S" coils together to form a heart shape.

Arrange hearts around the edge of the heart 3-D Keeper with the small ends toward the center. To complete the inner heart shape, roll 1" strips into loose glued coils and use for filler between small ends of hearts. Glue all shapes in place. Create the center heart in the same manner as the outside hearts using 6" lengths of quilling paper.

Jan Williams

GALLERY

As you can see, paper—that most basic of scrapbooking supplies—is also the most versatile, taking on a different personality each time it is cut, folded, layered, torn, woven, laced or rolled. The scrapbook artists featured in this book have taken paper from flat to fabulous with simple creative paper techniques. We're sure that their art will inspire you to experiment with your own creative paper techniques. Be sure to send us a photograph of your masterpiece!

By a Nose louvers, Torrey Miller

Ryan in Nana's Garden
kirigami, Sharon Moore

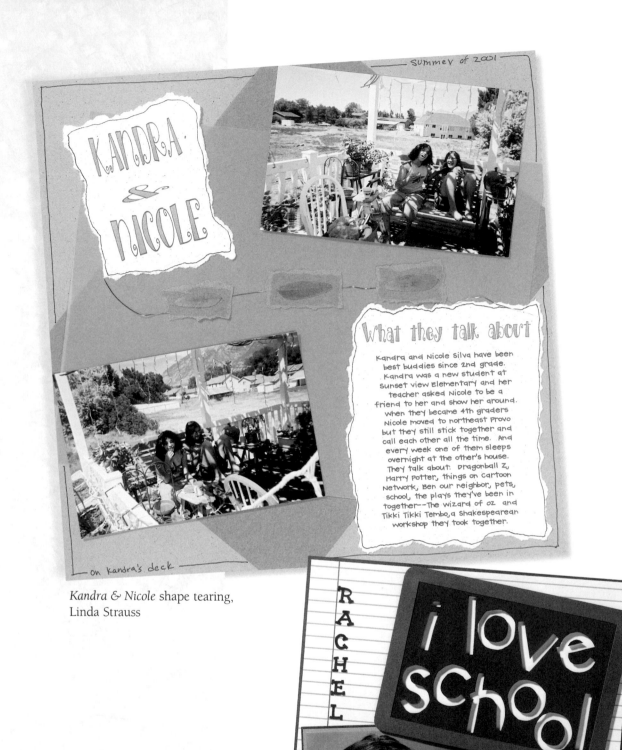

summer of 2001

KANDRA & NICOLE

What they talk about

Kandra and Nicole Silva have been best buddies since 2nd grade. Kandra was a new student at Sunset View Elementary and her teacher asked Nicole to be a friend to her and show her around. When they became 4th graders Nicole moved to northeast Provo but they still stick together and call each other all the time. And every week one of them sleeps overnight at the other's house. They talk about: Dragonball Z, Harry Potter, things on cartoon Network, Ben our neighbor, pets, school, the plays they've been in together--The wizard of oz and Tikki Tikki Tembo, a Shakespearean workshop they took together.

on kandra's deck

Kandra & Nicole shape tearing, Linda Strauss

RACHEL

i love school

grade 1

I Love School multiple-layer die cuts, Kelly Angard

Batter Up! quilled image accents,
Jan Williams

Olivia freestyle quilling,
Jan Williams

Everafter shape tearing,
Linda Strauss

Heritage Wedding diamond
bargello frame, Kelly Angard

A Visit With Grandpa & Grandma
random bargello quilt,
Stacey Shigaya

The Key to Happiness
assemblage, Erikia Ghumm

Hunter single-layer cutting,
Erikia Ghumm

Bathing Beauty quilling over
stenciled design, Jan Williams

PATTERNS

Use these helpful patterns to complete scrapbook pages featured in this book. Enlarge by percentage shown and photocopy the patterns. When transferring patterns to your paper of choice (see page 13), be sure to note solid, continuous lines for cut lines and dotted lines for fold lines.

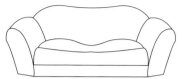

Page 6 Paper tole sofa (380%)

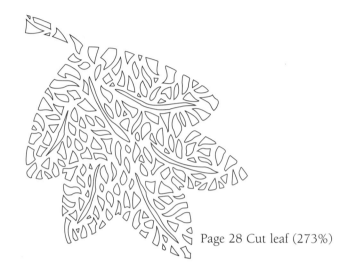

Page 28 Cut leaf (273%)

Page 44 Oval iris frame (210%)

Page 47 Rectangular iris frame (205%)

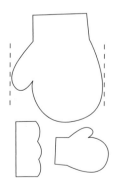

Page 52 Paper chain mittens (210%)

Page 54 Paper chain snowman
(181% for frame; 300% for border)

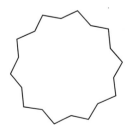

Page 56 Kirigami snowflake windows
(151%)

Page 60 Kirigami heart frame (338%)

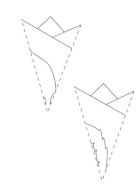

Page 62 Kirigami poinsettia & leaf (588%)

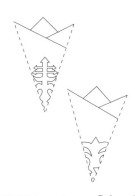

Page 63 Kirigami snowflakes (588%)

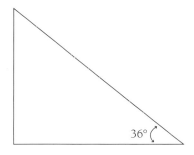

Pages 61-63
36° triangle for napkin fold (253%)

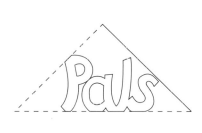

Page 64 Kirigami "Pals" (360%)

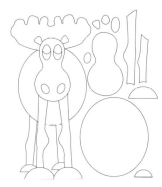

Page 76 Shape tearing moose (628%)

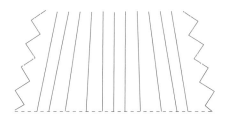

Page 96 Folded symmetrical loom (523%)

Page 98 Random curved loom (580%)

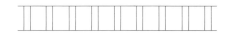

Page 102 Woven laced border (500%)

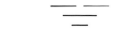

Page 104 Dutch-inspired flower (170%)

Page 104 Dutch-inspired hearts (230%)

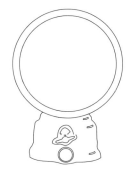

Page 117 Quilling gum-ball machine (460%)

Additional instructions & credits

Cover
Experiment with combining different paper craft techniques on one page for a stunning effect. This page features both louvers and paper tole for a dazzling effect. Papers used: Karen Foster, Paper Adventures, Scrap Ease. Photos Rick Cottrell, Deborah Knapp, MaryJo Regier

Page 6 Sibling Revelry
This page features a louvered window with a paper-torn and wrapped frame and a paper tole sofa. Papers: Colors by Design, Magenta, Making Memories, PrintWorks. See pattern for sofa on page 124. Photos Brenda Martinez

Pages 48-50 Pinch pleat

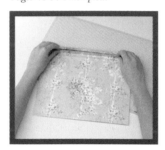

5 PINCH PLEAT To form the second row of pleats on the page, use a pencil and metal straight-edge ruler to draw parallel lines, alternating at ⅝" and ⅜" intervals, across the back of patterned paper. Score lines with a bone folder and ruler. Use both hands to "pinch" paper, coaxing scored lines up into a peak that can be folded to resemble an accordion fold. Continue until entire page is pleated.

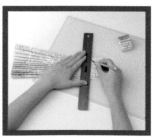

6 Cut 1" strips, vertically, using a craft knife and straightedge ruler, making sure to slice down upon the folds and not up against folds. Miter corners (see step 4 on page 50) and add tape adhesive to the back before mounting pleated strips on page atop box pleat border.

Page 50 Raised box pleat

1 Follow steps 1 through 4 on pages 49 and 50 for making box pleat border strips. Instead of adhering tape adhesive to back of strips to keep pleats in place, apply self-adhesive foam spacers to the backside of border strip on alternating sections of folds as shown. Flip the border over and mount to outer edges of the page.

Pages 66-67 Patterned paper tole

4 Adhere curled pieces atop sil-houetted butterflies, matching patterns and designs, with ⅛" self-adhesive foam spacers.

5 Mount paper tole elements atop their duplicate image on background paper with additional self-adhesive foam spacers, allowing some to overlap onto photos and title block.

Pages 56-57 Kirigami windows

1. Fold paper in half.

2. Fold paper in half again.

3. Trace shapes randomly, overlapping partial shapes atop fold lines.

Page 60 Kirigami heart frame

1. Start with 8½ x 11" paper.

2. Fold C and D to A and B, and crease.

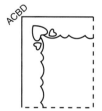

3. Fold BD to AC, folding paper in half again.

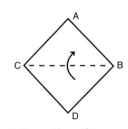

4. Transfer pattern (page 125) to folded paper, matching up fold lines; cut.

Pages 61-63 Kirigami poinsettias & snowflakes

1. Start with an 8½" square of paper. Fold D to A, folding in half to form triangle.

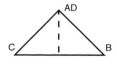

2. Fold B to C; just crease at lower, center point.

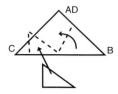

3. Photocopy and size 36° triangle pattern on page 125; transfer to cardstock and cut out. Place triangle on center point of folded paper triangle. Fold B toward AD along upper edge of 36° triangle; remove cardstock triangle.

4. Fold right edge of paper to edge of previous fold.

5. Flip folded paper over. Fold C over to line up with left edge fold.

Page 64 Personalized kirigami

1. Start with a 12" square of paper. Fold D to A diagonally to form a triangle.

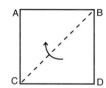

2. Fold B to C, folding triangle in half.

3. Fold AD to BC, folding triangle in half again.

4. Flip folded triangle over and rotate so that folded edges fall on the left and lower sides before tracing letters on folds to cut.

Sources

The following companies manufacture products featured in this book. Please check your local retailers to find these materials. In addition, we have made every attempt to properly credit the items mentioned in this book. We apologize to any company that we have listed incorrectly or the sources were unknown, and we would appreciate hearing from you.

3L Corp. (800) 828-3130

3M Stationery (800) 364-3577

All My Memories (888) 553-1998

All Night Media (800) 782-6733

Amy's Magic (724) 845-1748

Anna Griffin, Inc. (888) 817-8170

Art Accents (360) 733-8989

Artistic Wire Ltd.™ (630) 530-7567

Autumn Leaves (800) 588-6707

Bazzill Basics Paper (480) 558-8557

Beary Patch Wholesale, Inc. (877) 327-2111

Bo-Bunny Press (wholesale only) (801) 771-4010

Caren's Crafts. (805) 520-9635

Carl Mfg. USA, Inc. (800) 257-4771

Carolee's Creations (435) 563-1100

Colorbök, Inc. (wholesale only) (800) 366-4660

Colors By Design (800) 832-8436

Color Wheel Company, The (541) 929-7526

Crafter's Workshop, The (877) 272-3037

Craf-T Products (507) 235-3996

Creative Imaginations (800) 942-6487

Creative Keepsakes (888) 247-5282

Creative Memories® (800) 468-9335

C-Thru® Ruler Company, The (800) 243-8419

Cut-It-Up™ (530) 389-2233

Daisy Doodle (contact information unknown)

Deluxe Cuts (480) 497-9005

D.J. Inkers™ (800) 325-4890

DMC Corp. (973) 589-0606

DMD Industries, Inc. (800) 805-9890

Doodlebug Design Inc.™ (801) 524-0050

Dover Publications (800) 223-3130

EK Success™ Ltd. (800) 524-1349

Ever After Scrapbook Company (800) 646-0010

Family Treasures, Inc.® (800) 413-2645

Fiskars, Inc. (800) 950-0203

Frances Meyer, Inc.® (800) 372-6237

Glue Dots International (wholesale only) (888) 688-7131

Hallmark Cards, Inc. (800) 425-6275

Hero Arts® Rubber Stamps (wholesale only) (800) 822-4376

Hot Off The Press, Inc. (800) 227-9595

Imaginations, Inc. (877) 327-5467

Impress Rubber Stamps (206) 901-9101

Inspire Graphics (877) 472-3427

K & Company (888) 244-2083

Karen Foster Design (801) 451-9779

Lake City Craft Company (417) 725-8444

Lion Brand Yarn (800) 258-9276

Magenta Rubber Stamps (800) 565-5254

Making Memories (800) 286-5263

McGill Inc. (800) 982-9884

me & my BIG ideas (wholesale only) (949) 589-4607

Memory Muse Designs, LLC (503) 287-7952

Microsoft www.microsoft.com

Mrs. Grossman's Paper Company (800) 429-4549

My Mind's Eye™, Inc. (801) 298-3709

Nature's Pressed (800) 850-2499

Northern Spy (wholesale only) (530) 620-7430

NRN Designs (wholesale only) (800) 421-6958

On the Surface (847) 675-2520

Paper Adventures® (800) 727-0699

Paper Company™, The (800) 426-8989

Paper House Productions (800) 255-7316

Plaid Enterprises, Inc. (800) 842-4197

Pebbles in My Pocket® (800) 438-8153

Pressed Petals (800) 748-4656

PrintWorks (800) 854-6558

Provo Craft® (888) 588-3545

Punch Bunch, The (wholesale only) (254) 791-4209

Puzzle Mates™ (888) 595-2887

Ranger Industries, Inc. (800) 244-2211

Robin's Nest Press, The (wholesale only) (435) 789-5387

Sakura of America (800) 776-6257

Sandylion Sticker Designs (800) 387-4215

Scrapbook Wizard™, The (801) 947-0019

Scrap Ease® (800) 642-6762

Scrap Pagerz™ (435) 645-0696

Scrappin' Dreams (417) 831-1882

Sonburn, Inc. (800) 527-7505

Stamp Doctor, The (208) 286-7644 www.stampdoctor.com

Stampa Rosa, Inc. (800) 554-5755

Stampendous!® (wholesale only) (800) 869-0474

Stamping Staion Inc. (801) 444-3828

Stampin' Up!® (800) 782-6787

Strathmore Papers (800) 628-8816

Westrim Crafts (800) 727-2727

Wordsworth Memories (719) 282-3495

Wübie Prints (888) 256-0107

Artist Index

Photo Contributors

Professional Photographers

Page 60 Kirigami heart frame

Mardel Photography
9424 S. Union Square
Sandy, Utah 84070

Bibliography

The History of Paper Cutting
fascinating-folds.com/papercuts/papercuttinghistory.htm

The Bargello Page
locutus.ucr.edu/~cathy/barg/barg.html

Index